THE POETS OF PRAGUE

Czech Poetry Between the Wars

ALFRED FRENCH

THE POETS OF PRAGUE
Czech Poetry Between the Wars

London
OXFORD UNIVERSITY PRESS
NEW YORK TORONTO
1969

Oxford University Press, Ely House, London W.1

GLASGOW NEW YORK TORONTO MELBOURNE WELLINGTON
CAPE TOWN SALISBURY IBADAN NAIROBI LUSAKA ADDIS ABABA
BOMBAY CALCUTTA MADRAS KARACHI LAHORE DACCA
KUALA LUMPUR SINGAPORE HONG KONG TOKYO

Printed in Great Britain by
NEILL AND CO. LTD., EDINBURGH

PREFACE

I wish to thank all those who have helped me so generously with their encouragement, their advice, and in many cases their unpublished recollections, while I was preparing this book. I am indebted to members of the Caroline University of Prague, and of the Institute of Czech Literature at Strahov; above all to the Czech writers themselves. This book is a small return for the friendship I have received in Prague.

Most of the work was written at my home in Australia. By the generosity of Adelaide University I was able to revisit Czechoslovakia in 1962 and 1966, where the literary sources of the period were made entirely available to me. Back in Prague in August 1968 I was preparing the work finally for publication when, for the second time in my experience, the city passed into alien military occupation: among the first buildings to be seized by the soldiers was that of the Writers' Club. So ended that last, wonderful summer of hope.

The winter is long in Bohemia; but those who know Prague remember the white lilac, whose appearance in May is traditionally the sign of a new summer to come. Perhaps one day we shall see it again.

University College,   A.F.
Cambridge.   March 1969

v

CONTENTS

1 Introduction   1

2 The Proletarian Phase   8

3 Poetism   29

4 The End of the Carnival   43

5 Poems of the Night   60

6 The Search   77

7 Interval for Surrealism   91

8 Put out the Lights!   109

  Select Bibliography   121

  Index   125

ILLUSTRATIONS

facing page

1 Contemporary caricatures by A. Hoffmeister:

   (a) 'The Discussion'   54

   (b) 'The Avantgarde'   54

2 Cover, designed by J. Štyrský, of Nezval's collection, *Pantomime* 55

3 'The poet-clown'   70

4 Cover, designed by Karel Teige, of Seifert's collection, *On Waves of Radio*   71

1

INTRODUCTION

AT the close of the nineteenth century the political and social atmosphere in the Czech lands was one of increasing disillusion. The goal of national liberation appeared no nearer; and the programme of gradual self-determination and political compromise encountered stiffening resistance from Vienna. At the same time, trust in material progress was being eroded by financial crises, and the theoretical foundations of laissez-faire economics questioned by socialist teachings. Within this depressing social context the lot of the writer and the artist seemed to be reaching its lowest ebb. At a time when municipal offices were designed to look like renaissance palaces, and railways stations equipped with baroque facades; when mass-produced industrial goods were ousting craftsmanship and photography apparently taking over the functions of graphic art, the rift between the artist and his public appeared to be temporarily unbridgeable. Feeling themselves ignored and rejected by society at large, poets and painters accepted their role as a race apart, and exaggerated their isolation by their whole style of life. The artist who could not sell his pictures, the poet declaiming his verses to a narrow circle of seedy acquaintances, found solace in their eccentricity, and prided themselves on their ability to shock middle-class opinion. Against the solid moral standards of bourgeois respectability they reacted by posing as the addicts of free love and satanism: prevented by circumstances from living as they would have liked, they celebrated the cult of decay and death. They thought of themselves as the lost generation, and following the French model they called themselves the Decadents.

The fact that the century was drawing to its close acquired a sort of mystical significance. Writers believed, or affected to believe, that their world was doomed. The individual could retreat only into himself and find a private salvation in art. Writers fired their broadsides against society in general and their elders in particular: they attacked relativism in philosophy, philistinism and eclecticism in art, and opportunism in politics. Czech literature became more cosmopolitan in outlook, and its lyric poets were increasingly subject to the influence of the modern French and Anglo-American schools; the work of Baudelaire, Verlaine, and Whitman left an enduring impression on Czech lyric poetry. It had been a traditional role of Czech literature to keep alive and undiluted the national spirit, and nothing irritated the modernists more than what they regarded as the sentimental nationalism of their elders. A manifesto published in 1895 and signed by an eminent group of young writers declares: 'Gloomy auspices have presided at the growth of the present generation. Suffocated by empty phrases, nauseated by Slavic mottoes and patriotic anthems, we have opened our eyes. With scepticism we have looked upon our fathers. A sorry sight.'

Since the members of the group were, above all, individualists, the paths of protest which they followed were correspondingly diverse. Perhaps the high-water mark of the Decadents in the field of poetry was reached by Karel Hlaváček in his gloomy epic *Mstivá Kantilena* (*Song of Vengeance*), a book first printed in an edition of only 100 copies. Machar and O. Březina both turned from the abhorred spectacle of contemporary society, the former to the themes of classical antiquity, the latter to a metaphysical dream-world. Realism was represented by P. Bezruč, whose poems of social protest at times verge upon hymns of hate; and by S. K. Neumann who graduated from Decadence and anarchy to naturalism and Marxism. But it was perhaps in the field of literary criticism that the men of the 1890s had their most lasting effect. The work of J. Karásek, T. G. Masaryk, and above all of F. X. Šalda raised Czech criticism to the level of an independent genre and set standards that were to discipline the writing of generations to come.

Upon this scene of intellectual ferment fell the shock of the First World War, dwarfing for the moment problems and divisions which had seemed to be critical. It is commonly observed of the Czechs that they cease from their internecine recriminations only when common catastrophe threatens to engulf them all. After 1914 the ranks began to close, and amid the struggle for survival the fulminations of the artists seemed in retrospect somewhat esoteric. As so often in the hard times of the past, Czech writers turned back to tradition and to the cult of their native soil. Forgetting his haughty and Satanic pose, S. K. Neumann drew from the Moravian countryside inspiration for his book *Kniha lesů, vod, a strání* (*A Book of Woods, Streams and Slopes*); while

Sova and Šrámek yielded to the spell of the motherland, conceived in erotic tones. With the progress of the war political control from Vienna became harsher, and writer after writer was silenced or imprisoned. At that time V. Dyk expressed the voice of Czech patriotism in the warning of the motherland to her sons: '*Opustíš-li mne, nezahynu —Opustíš-li mne, zahyneš!*' ('If you leave me, I live on—if you leave me, you will die'). Pacifism and reviving nationalism were motifs of Czech wartime writing which seemed to be drawing the parties and the generations back into a common front.

Meanwhile beyond the frontiers a group of exiles headed by T. G. Masaryk was lobbying the allied powers for a programme of independence for the Czech lands as part of any post-war settlement. In France and Italy deserters from the Austrian armies were forming the new Czech legion to re-enter the struggle on the side of the allies: in Russia, after the March revolution of 1917, the Provisional Government actively co-operated to assist the Czechs to join their fellows on the Western front. This period of official Russo-Czech co-operation was terminated by the October revolution, when Trotsky ordered the Czech units to be disarmed, and the civil war closed their westward exit. So began the eastward movement of the Czech legion: officially neutral in the civil war and advised by French officers, they forced their way across Siberia to Vladivostok and finally reached home with Russian wives and gold, and with definite opinions about revolution. They were to be for some time the only sizable group with practical experience of the new Russia, and the views of some of their leaders clashed with the idealist attitude of the young socialists at home. They formed an important pressure group in the new state and later produced an interesting prose literature based on their wartime experiences.

News of the Bolshevik revolution was received by the Czechs with excitement, but with mixed feelings. The nationalists had placed all their hopes on the prosecution of the war against the Germans, and the Russian withdrawal filled them with dismay. On the other hand there was rejoicing for the victory of the socialist cause; and many, especially among the younger generation, fervidly ranged themselves in sympathy with the Bolsheviks and saw in their victory a new hope for mankind. To the humanists, too, the war appeared as such a crime against humanity that it could be understood only if it resulted in some great advance for humanity as a sort of atonement for the boundless suffering it had caused. The revolution offered a hope of such advance, and was welcomed eagerly, even by those who had not before been of markedly socialist persuasion. The impending collapse of the Austrian imperial system, and the sweeping away of the old order in Russia, appeared as part of a world movement to replace a state of things which had outlived its time, by a new era of hope for liberated mankind. The first Czechoslovak president himself described the epoch as one of world revolution, of which the war was only a part.

In October 1918, as the broken regiments of Austria were streaming in disarray back from the front, the new republic was proclaimed in Prague. Thus was demonstrated in a material way the conviction that for the Czechs and Slovaks a whole epoch had closed and a new era begun. The new state was made possible by the energetic lobbying and intrigue of the exile group in Paris; by the services of the Czech Maffia to French Military Intelligence during the war; by the efforts and example of the Legionaries abroad; by the sympathy of President Wilson for small nations; above all, by the strategy of Clemenceau to encircle Germany and to divide her from Bolshevik Russia. The climate of opinion among Czech thinkers was for an entirely new deal, as was recognized by Masaryk himself, who rejected the possibility that national liberation might mean merely the exchange of one ruling group for another, and regarded the national struggle as part of the wider social struggle. The new state was conceived in the spirit of French revolutionary tradition and wrote upon its banners not only the motto of liberty, fraternity, equality, but also the ideals of the medieval Hussites. The new beginning was to mark not only a break with a discredited past but a continuity with all that was best in Czech protestant tradition.

But the ideals and slogans of the new-born state hardly corresponded with political realities. The year 1918 was in fact the beginning not of a millennium of brotherhood and peace but of economic struggle and military danger. Once the transference of power had taken place and the provisional government had been installed, the need of the day was for stability not revolution. The official ideology of the new state was liberal and democratic, rejecting all extremism. The first year of independence in fact saw an unprecedented programme of social reform which reflected the radical fervour of the day. On the other hand, official denunciation of imperialism was somewhat muted, in deference to Czechoslovakia's Western allies: internally and externally it was a time of hard bargaining and political compromise; and the radicals, victorious at the first elections, soon found themselves out-manoeuvred. The national liberation changed many things, but its achievements did not

accord with all the extravagant hopes put upon it, and the wave of subsequent disillusion was correspondingly intense.

A painful contradiction soon appeared between the official desire for
an entirely fresh start, and the need for administrative continuity. At
the very moment when tradition was being rejected, it was on traditional
and historical grounds that the frontiers of the new state were being
drawn at Versailles. The contrast between the hope and the reality,
between the idealist and the realistic outlook, at times shaded into a new
clash between the generations. The soldiers who returned home as
heroes found themselves to be almost strangers to the sons who had
grown up during their absence. The politicians who returned as libera-
tors had grown old in the struggle and found themselves identified with
the era from which they had emerged. Kramář, hero of the resistance
and leader of the so-called Young Czechs, was bewildered to find himself rejected by the electorate. The years of war had split the generations
and exposed an ugly rift which time seemed only to widen.

This rift went wider than the antipathy between left-wing youth and
conservative age, as can be seen from the attitude of so firm a conservative as the young Peroutka, later to become a pillar of the Establishment. In 1922 he published a book, *Jací jsme* (*As We Really Are*), in
which he set out to demolish the pretensions of his elders. Speaking for
his contemporaries he declared his total disinterest in Czech history and
the struggle for independence: the traditional image of the Czech people
as idyllic, humanist, heroic, protestant, was an illusion by which a poor
and dependent people had tried to romanticize its harsh situation. Now
that the illusion was no longer necessary, the Czechs should see themselves as they were—petty nationalists, half-hearted Catholics, sentimental liberals, and born compromisers, whose humanism was a
cloak to cover their sense of national weakness.

The divisions of the Czech people again appeared to be widening at a
time when the survival of the new state required maximum co-
operation. One lesson of the war had been the dependence of the
individual upon his fellows: trench warfare had taught men the need
for mutual support amid common danger, and the truth that the mass
can survive where the isolated individual goes down. Post-war
political creeds put much emphasis upon the solidarity and discipline
of the group, and in art the problem of the individual's relationship to
the mass became an important motif. Whereas the artist of the 1890s
had stressed his aloofness and shunned the vulgar herd, the writer of
the twenties tended rather to identify himself with the crowd. In the

radical spirit of the time writers proclaimed their allegiance to the legions of the poor and the oppressed, and in spirit marched with them to the barricades. A symbol of their collective struggle, the proletarian worker, now appeared in literature as the hero of the new age. At the same time the poet began to see himself as a prophet of his people and the voice of their conscience. After the chaos of war, when the avalanche had swept away familiar landmarks and all values were in question, a new note of messianism appeared, as men sought for security in some new creed. Having lost all faith in religion men fervently embraced the gospel of Marxism and saw the new saviour as the leader of the revolutionary masses.

Apart from this stream stood writers more deeply rooted in tradition, who looked with shock, amusement, or approval upon such youthful fervour. Men like Březina, Machar, and Dyk found little point of contact with their youthful fellows; their work was permeated with other convictions and values, to which they remained true. Between the generations, cut off from the tradition of the old, yet not sharing in the intoxication of the new, lay an intermediate group, the so-called pragmatists, including K. Čapek. Their strength lay in prose rather than poetry and they came to be regarded almost as official spokesmen for the regime. Of them it was said that they loved the whole world and believed in nothing; and the accusation, though not entirely justified, exemplifies the tragedy of their isolation.

The pre-war and post-war generations were spanned by writers like Neumann, Šrámek, and Šalda, who were all, in their fashion, models and mentors for the young. But the youthful writers felt and revealed a homogeneity which marked them off as a separate group. The war had robbed them of their later childhood and they clung to their youth as though they feared to be identified with age. Despising the apparent hypocrisy and opportunism of their elders they proclaimed the sanctity of truth, and often felt that they had a monopoly of it. They questioned everything—even reason itself—and when logic failed them, they turned to the irrational and the cult of nonsense. Their rebellious manner provoked a host of reprisals from their elders, and they were easily hurt. They were aggressively modern, and absorbed every modernist trend from Russian Proletkult to Italian Futurism, from Dadaism to Surrealism. Their eccentricity and iconoclasm scandalized the critics and lost them many would-be friends: they were extremist in everything they did, and quarrelled violently among themselves. They were full of frustrated energy and weighed down by frustrated hopes, for the times were against them. They did not inherit the earth nor witness the millennium, and the extravagant banners under which they marched in cheerful disarray were to lead them not to a promised land but to a fresh catastrophe, which was itself a new beginning.

2

THE PROLETARIAN PHASE

IN 1918 ended the Austrian imperial censorship of news and literature in the Czech lands. Down came the barriers which had for four years isolated Czech readers from French and Anglo-American literary influences. The result was a lively increase in the demand both for information and for creative writing on the part of a public which was starved for foreign news and fashions, and which felt itself caught up in the exciting climate of change. Czech newspapers expanded their circulations and widened their coverage to include literary reviews and commentaries, often contributed by the leading writers of the day. In gallant competition with such formidable rivals a crop of new literary journals sprouted on all sides, usually of a very brief life-span. Among the most important of these were *Kmen* (*Stem*), edited by F. X. Šalda, later by Neumann; *Cesta* (*Voyage*), a journal of wide interests edited by M. Rutte; and *Červen* (*June*), founded as a platform for young Marxist writers and edited by the energetic Neumann. The number of small local or student journals devoted to new writing was phenomenal, and it became the ambition of each freshly formed literary group to have its own journal as a sounding box for the views of its members and an outlet for their original work.

At that time literary circles were enthusing over the wartime poetry of Šrámek and Neumann: their books, *Splav* (*The Sluice*) and *Nové zpěvy* (*New Songs*) respectively, represented a phase of deliberate naturalism, when writers took as their province the most simple and earthy of subjects. Amid the uncertainties and dangers of war, things which had hitherto been taken for granted suddenly became endearing to men who realized how precarious was their hold upon them; thus was restored to the trite object its lost mystery, and to men the feeling that even to be alive was precious beyond expression. It was poetry which would soon cloy once the situation passed away, but in the first flush of the post-war world, when life stretched enticingly ahead and everything seemed possible, it was heady wine to the young, determined to wipe

8

academism out of art and to return to its roots. At the same time exhibitions of modern painting were beginning to reflect childish motifs and exploit the charm of bold crudeness in technique. It was the aim of sophisticated artists to break down accepted forms, and to paint like a gifted child. In reaction against Impressionism, which had so perfected representational art as virtually to close the door on further advance, painters called themselves Expressionists, and deliberately avoided representational fidelity. Aiming to strip away incidental phenomena from the subject and reveal the essence below, they distorted nature; as a caricature exaggerates in order to express humour or satire, so they exaggerated to express pity, fear, or horror. In Western Europe Expressionism as a style quickly spread from painting to literature, combining with the desire of writers to go back to first principles. It was partly the feeling that a new world was coming to replace the old; but to see the new world all must become as children. Hence Expressionist literature in France and Germany combined the motifs of primitivism with political evangelism: the new poetry aimed to gain an immediate reaction by shocking the reader and by appealing not to the reason but to the heart. Its deliberate disintegration of art forms reflected its revolt against the whole organization of society, and it combined apocalyptic visions of horror with the idea of the fraternity of suffering humanity. Every poem became a spiritual vision, every emotion larger than life: one of its favourite motifs was the adventure of a lost spirit in search of a dream, a dream of harmony which could be glimpsed or recalled only by a child. Among the most distinguished writers of this school were Arcos, Duhamel, and Vildrac, but its influence extended deeply into modern art generally, and Brod, Jacob, Cocteau, Apollinaire, and Picasso all at some time came under its spell. The Czech Expressionists were never so extreme as their French and German counterparts: in spite of their wild talk of anarchy they preserved the continuity of their literature and, for the most part, adopted the constructive rather than the destructive aspects of Expressionism. If they came to destroy, they came also to build, and they were filled with the desire to translate the dream into reality. Determined to end the old ways in art and in life, they rejected the isolation of art from life, and plunged into the struggle as they saw it, eager to use literature as their tool.

During the war a young poet, Josef Hora, had made his debut with a slim book entitled simply *Básně* (*Poems*). The book had caused no sensation; it was full of ideas and impressions, but was too intellectual and reflective to be a success as lyric poetry. Hora however had a genuine talent for combining romantic and tragic motifs, and intimations of his later mature work were contained in this book. The poem *'Kdo zpívá tu píseň'* ('Who is it Singing that Song') begins:

> Who is it singing that song
>   of a heady night in Spring?
> from every side it swells
> like the rustle of bursting trees,
> like the sobbing of bells.
>
> The murmur of far-away tempests,
>   the march of troops through a land
> filled with vast uncertainty,
> a prayer to a god who died, resound
> through that crazy melody . . .[1]

The poem is an accurate forecast of his development—restlessly searching for a richer quality in life, he finds a melancholy fulfilment only in the search itself.

> You will dream no more of peace
>   in the shelter of joy recalled,
> you will seek no more
> in gathering love, and wisdom, and wealth,
> to live from their store.
>
> And always you will hear it,
>   the song of the heady nights,
> as it builds new fates, fusing old loves spent.
> And always you will hear it, in towns, amid loneliness,
> upon fresh magic's scent.
>
> And you will never more be happy
>   as you nurse it in your heart,
> for it no peace will give:
> you will laugh and cry; you will love and hate.
> You will live . . .[2]

---

[1] Kdo zpívá tu píseň závratné jarní noci,
   rostoucí se všech stran,
   znící jak kypících stromů šum chvíli
   a chvíli jak nářek hran?

In 1920 Hora published two new books of verse. In the first, *Strom v květu* (*A Tree in Blossom*), he portrays the bustle of war-time Prague: in the fashion of the time the poet yields to the fascination of the technical age, loving its power but sensing its dangers. But, again in the fashion of the day, he turns back for security to his native countryside. Hora was much addicted to the love-hate relationship; feeling both pull and counter-pull on his feelings. While he felt in some sense exiled when away from the country, on the other hand he longed to lose himself in the unity of the crowd, and to identify himself with the surge of social protest. In '*Sodom a Gomora*' he contrasts the luxury of the city shop-windows with the moral poverty and degradation of the profiteers who patronize them. In '*Kristus na rozcestí*' ('Christ at the Crossroads') the theme is the alienation of man from man in urban life. In *Proměna* ('Change') the theme is metaphysical: there is no stable principle at work in the world save change itself; amid the shifting stream man finds an anchor only in himself. Begotten by his passions and fed by the earth he soars like a tree to heaven, drawn on only by his dreams ('*Plný den*'— 'Full Day').

Hora was a poet of unending tensions, pulled this way and that between town and country, the grey North of home and the exotic South of his imagination, the gay mask of the world and the shadow of social tragedy, the loneliness of the individual and the security of the crowd. In his next book *Pracující den* (*Working Day*) there is greater emphasis on the social motif. The atmosphere which he tries to catch is that of

---

Šum bouří vzdálených, nejistota všeho
v kraji, jímž vojska jdou,
modlitba k bohu, jenž zemřel,
zní hudbou tou šílenou . . .

[2] Již nebudeš sníti o míru v závětří starého štěstí,
již nebudeš chtít,
shromáždiv lásku, bohatství a moudrost,
z jich zásob žít . . .

Budeš ji stále slyšet, píseň závratných nocí,
zestárlé tavit lásky, nové osudy kout,
budeš ji stále slyšet, městy i samotami
za novým kouzlem dout . . .

A nebudeš nikdy šťasten, živě ji v srdci svém kletém,
a nenalezneš klid . . .
Budeš jen plakat a smát se, milovat, nenávidět,
budeš jen žít—

the urban working class, and to suit his subject he cuts down the philosophical content of his ideas and the subtlety of his style. Industrial work by its repetition drives man into the likeness of the machine he tends: in the poem '*Poledne*' ('Midday') the theme is the moment of freedom and truth, when the worker leaves his machine briefly to become again a man among men. In this blessed interlude he hears the voice of the sirens calling him to freedom, but they are drowned by the more compelling voice of the factory siren. On the one hand there is slavery to the machine, on the other the reality of unemployment: the poem '*Nezoufej!*' ('Do not Despair!') portrays the helplessness of the industrial worker. Lost himself, he sees around him other lost men; as they sink beneath the water they mutely stretch out their arms for help, to him, who has none to give. The isolation of the worker reflects Hora's own feeling of spiritual isolation: the only hope lies in the collective movement of the crowd. The poet glimpses their strength, but the act of faith is strained, and he easily lapses into rhetoric. Hora was always better at posing a dilemma than offering a solution which he felt himself to be ingenuous.

With a heightening sensitivity to life comes increasing sensitivity to death. In '*Hřbitov*' ('The Cemetery') a child is playing among the tombstones; the stone becomes a symbol of life, not death, to the poet who clutches it like a drowning man, fearful to lose the life whose gloom he feels. The feeling that he is condemned goes everywhere with him and makes him an exile on the face of the earth. The towering works of nature mock man's illusion of mastery over her, and touch the pilgrims with the icy breath of annihilation.

The liberation of industrial man is conceived as a spiritual rebirth: as the spring smooths away the cruel winter, so the revolution will bring sunshine back into the world. As the Mayday procession moves through Prague, the demonstrators sway like ripe corn: to lead them must come a modern Messiah of the workers. The poem '*Dělnická Madona*' ('Working-class Madonna') pictures the new nativity:

> A witness would have seen damp walls,
> a basement's dingy half-light, on a bed
> a woman, who had borne a son of man.
>
> For incense, see, the smoking stove,
> the mean food's smell, the palliasse
> with a swarm of children who could sing
> a Christmas hymn of poverty.

How coarse, how drab you are, Madonna! on
your hands the criss-cross of blue veins,
your forehead harshly lined with abstinence, dried lips—
the words of love long since
swilled down the throat of poverty.

And the three wise men? They shunned that house;
they had no gift left over for your child:
the star of heaven had led them much astray.
They scattered all their gold, their myrrh, their kindly smile,
to well-warmed homes and bedrooms soft.
Rich men themselves, they went among their kind.

And Bethlehem
is full of poor, and tattered, shoeless folk,
the blind, the sick, the lost . . .
How laboured is your breath, your beauty gone from you:
what bitter milk the wonder-child sucks from your veins!
And yet believe!
when thirty years are past He will ride to town,
the gospel of revolt upon His lips,
proclaiming on the square that justice is at hand,
and arm the crowds, and set into their hands a dream—and steel—
and will not let Himself be crucified.

For His prayer shall be a deed.[1]

---

[1] Kdybys tam byl, vlhké zdivo bys viděl,
špinavé šero podsklepí, lůžko a v něm ženu,
jež porodila z člověka.

Ach, kadidlo! Viděl bys kouřící kamna,
zápach chudého oběda bys pocítil,
hromádku dětí, jež zazpívaly by ti koledu bídy,
uzřel bys na slamníku.

Madono! Jak hrubá jsi! Jak odkvetlá!
Splet' zamodralých na rukou žil,
vzdor odříkání pod čelem, rty vyschlé—
a slova lásky už dávno
pohltil chřtán bídy.

A tři králové! Vyhnuli se tomuto domu,
nestačilo jim darů pro tebe, ženo s dítětem.
Hvězda boží dala jim zabloudit.
Roztrousili své zlato, svou mast, svůj laskavý úsměv
po teplých příbytcích, měkkých ložnicích,
sami boháči, šli mezi své.

Although Hora was only twenty-seven years old when the war finished, the young poets of Prague who made their debut after the war regarded him as belonging to an older generation, and more as a guide than as one of themselves. Among the host of would-be writers and artists in Prague there was a group of young enthusiasts who used to meet informally at the Café Union. Children of their time, they were revolutionaries as a matter of course, and derided anything bourgeois, including their own government, which they regarded as a tool of French imperialism. They assumed that it would prove little more enduring than the Russian provisional government of Kerensky, and looked forward with pleasurable anticipation to the time when it would be swept aside by the full tide of revolution. Their talk was of Kropotkin and Bakunin; they expressed their contempt for Czech jingoism by anti-militarist songs, and their cosmopolitan culture by singing the *Internationale* in French. They were equally devoted to political extremism and avantgarde art.

To join this wild group came a model youth of a very different stamp, Jiři Wolker, who was introduced by his friend and former collaborator on a student journal, Z. Kalista.

Wolker, then nineteen, had come from the small town of Prostějov to the University in Prague. He was the product of a sound middle-class home of monumental respectability; he was a talented musician as well as a budding poet, and was the pride of his family. Unlike many secondary-school students he had never had to live in lodgings or fend for himself, but had studied at home, surrounded by family affection. Some of his student friends found his manner rather off-hand: he had plenty of reserve and no small confidence in himself. Wolker had the

A Betlém
je pln chudých, odraných, neobutých,
slepých, nemocných, pobloudilých—
ty tu dýcháš tak těžce, krása opadla s tebe,
dítě-zázrak pije hořké mléko tvých žil,
ale věř:
Až doroste třiceti let,
vjede do města s evangeliem odboje na rtech,
ohlásí na náměstí příchod spravedlnosti,
ozbrojí zástupy, sen i kov dá jim do ruky—
a nedá se ukřižovat.
Neboť' jeho modlitbou bude čin.

idea that he was of English descent and thought that his name (unfamiliar in Czech) was a corruption of the English 'Walker'; perhaps in consequence of this he was much interested in English literature and was familiar with the work of Oscar Wilde and Edgar Allan Poe. Although fond of Decadent poetry he detested any form of artistic eccentricity: he was very athletic and open air minded: he was a Catholic, and a member of the Sokol patriotic organization. It was at first sight difficult to imagine a more unlikely recruit for the Union group of café revolutionaries.

Since Wolker had moved to Prague, the harmonious tranquillity of his life hitherto came to an abrupt end. Although the old city fascinated him, he was dismayed by the squalid slums and the aimlessness of their inhabitants. He was startled, but impressed, by the rebelliousness and the brilliance of the Union group, and on his first visit he spoke hardly at all. Actually his main reservations, as quickly appeared, were for their views on art and literature rather than on politics. He had a natural sympathy for the downtrodden, no doubt partly due to his liberal upbringing, and his disgust at the conditions he found in Prague had prepared him for the radical views of his new acquaintances. He accepted their attitude of political revolution with all the enthusiasm of a convert, and because, unlike the rest, he had no trace of anarchy in his make-up, he brought to the group a welcome touch of self-discipline. In matters of art he believed himself to be a modernist; but in the provincial world of Prostějov the literature of the Decadents was still the latest thing. Wolker was much influenced by the work of Verlaine and Baudelaire, and his own juvenile poems were of that school. In Prague, however, he came into touch with much more recent trends, and in 1920 appeared a book which was to leave a great impress on Czech lyric poetry for years to come. It was K. Čapek's anthology of modern French poetry in translation, and it was something of a revelation to young writers, opening up new vistas and introducing them to recent Expressionist and Futurist verse. It was in the following summer that Wolker published his first book *Host do domu* (*A Guest into the Home*), comprising poems written since 1919.

As the Expressionists aimed to draw like children, so Wolker had written in the style of a child. The book was scattered with flowers, angels, saints and miracles, and inspired by a cult of innocence, wonder, and humility. In the world of Wolker the ordinary limitations of time and space were suspended, as in a dream or a fairy tale: the organizing principle was a mysterious harmony which reduced all things to the human category. In '*Žebráci*' ('Beggars') God comes to the door as a beggar, in '*Háj*' ('The Grove') He will come to supper. In '*Vzdálená milá*' ('The Faraway Lover') the moon and stars drop in to visit the poet, and at his request they sally forth to look for his girl. There is no death in this world; those who have ended their life rise up again in the trees of the cemetery and the flowers of the field. In Wolker's poems features of a familiar scene are regrouped into fresh combinations by a form of pictorial composition. A sickroom becomes a pond; the patient is held down by the weight of the bed to prevent her swimming to the window; her body is transparent like glass. A window in the poet's room becomes a glass ship which sails to far-away continents and returns gladly to the still-life of his possessions. His dreams are as violent and erotic as those of a child. As the horn calls to the hunt he gazes at the picture of the Virgin hanging up on his wall: at the kill he will pierce her breast with a lily, and when he returns home she will step down from the wall to wipe the sweat from his brow. He will come back from the wars with an open wound, into which his bride will plunge, and lose herself in fresh life. In '*Poutníci*' ('Pilgrims') the star of the nativity leads the three kings through a homely world, the foot-path to heaven. In the title poem of the book there is a new version of the nativity. The star leads the poet to a centre of suburban poverty, and upon the empty plates of a starving family he offers his own eyes. The sacrifice inspires a poem which lights the way of the pilgrims: the door of the house swings open, admitting the poet, and with him another, unseen guest—the God whom he had gone forth to seek.

The concluding piece of the book was a long poem, '*Svatý Kopeček*', the name of the village where Wolker used to spend his holidays; but the subject of the poem is Wolker himself. Based on the model of Apollinaire's '*La Zone*', which Wolker had read in Čapek's translation, the poem moves by the method of thought association among his memories of the past and his dreams of the future. Wolker sits at the deathbed of the woman who once tended his childish illnesses; now the roles are reversed, but there is no toy that will comfort her as she had comforted him. Before him rise up the images of his past life, including his youthful dreams, which live their own life into the future, confusing the layers of time. The world of the past, filtered through memory, confronts the world of the future, glimpsed in the dream, and the climax of recollection is reached when the poet takes up his violin, and links past with future by art. The sonata he plays portrays his past life, especially his artistic loves, and sounds an epitaph upon his cult of

Decadence in literature: he dedicates himself from now on to reality—
'Our kingdom is of this world'. The poet becomes the tongue of a great
bell, calling to all mankind, and he prays to the symbol of his childhood,
the standard of Svatý Kopeček, for strength to carry the faith of today
into the reality of tomorrow.

It has been said of the Decadents that they placed art before life: in
the realist school to which Wolker was pledging allegiance, life came
before art, which was a part of life, and subservient to its purposes. It
was at this time that Wolker began to be interested in the social function of art, and it was this that drew him to the school of which he
became the only real master in Czech literature, that of so-called
Proletarian poetry.

Hora had pointed the way for the new movement by his book
Pracující den (Working Day), which had emphasized the social, rather
than the naive and apocalyptic aspects of Expressionism. The appeal
of the latter style was of short duration, and its dangers of sentimentality
had already been shown by the poems of Wolker himself. In attempting
to escape from the trap of infantile romanticism and philosophical soul-
searching, writers sought more and more to identify themselves with
the crowd, to express the feelings and hopes of the masses in common
language, returning art to the common man. The cry of the nineteenth-
century avantgarde had been 'Art for art's sake', and in the twentieth
century art had in fact been divorced from its public, filling museums,
picture galleries, and libraries with goods which appealed only to a
minute section of the community. The aim of Czech post-war writers,
to link up again with a mass audience, was in line with their radical
political views. It also coincided with a shift in the Czech popular taste
in art, whereby the theatre began to lose its audience to the cinema, and
classical music to the exponents of negro jazz. The trend was to a new
form of primitivism, the romantic side of which was represented by the
cowboy epics of Eddie Polo and the throbbing drums of Dixieland.
It was the realistic aspect of this trend in art which was represented by
Proletarian literature. In order to recapture the ear of the common man,
art needed to avoid obscurity, and to be linked with his interests. Thus
Proletarian writers were led back to folk poetry, especially to the folk
ballad, except that the setting and substance of their poems was drawn
from the contemporary world of the urban proletariat. They were well
aware of the dangers of such literature, and avoided both the cult of
arty primitivism on the one hand, and the patronizing uplift of a would-
be Ruskin on the other. The aim of the Proletarian poets was not only

to write for the proletariat, but to see the world through its eyes—not, as it were, to look into the proletarian world from the outside, but to look outwards from it. But Proletarian poetry was not only an expression of social humanism and spiritual identification with the masses; it was also intended directly to assist their struggle. As art had once possessed a social function—the song that beats out the rhythm of marching men or of workers in the fields—so the new poetry was to sing the hymns of Marxist revolution. Its purpose was not to mirror life but to change it, not to describe but to prophesy and to inspire, even as the hymns of the early Christian fathers had inspired their followers.

Proletarian literature was thus definitely committed to a political cause, with all the dangers that this involved. The cause was social revolution; not the anarchy of the avantgardists but the disciplined movement of the socialists. The year 1920 had in fact been a bad one for the latter: after gaining a majority in the first national elections the socialist front had split over policy, when the left wing sought to affiliate the party to the Moscow International. The split brought about the fall of the government and the appointment of a caretaker administration under a bureaucrat from the old regime: an attempted general strike was broken by vigorous police action, and the would-be revolutionaries, bewildered and out-manoeuvred, found themselves left out in the cold. The new state, which had started out with such radical ideas, settled down into a mould of cautious respectability, borrowing its political faith and forms from modern France. It was not that the system was oppressive, but rather that the reality was so much at variance with the early ideals of social justice and Hussite fraternity. In this situation the ardent young reformers who had begun with such high hopes found cause only for anger and frustration. F. X. Šalda, looking back over these years, wrote in 1923: 'Some future Balzac will tell one day how dearly, with what betrayal of heart and spirit, with what moral bankruptcy and loss of reason, intellect and culture we have paid for the practical realization of our state . . . of the diluted, false translation of our heroes' intentions into the bad prose of today's liberal non-civilization.'

Such was the literary and political background of the Proletarian phase of Czech literature. A pioneer of the movement was Jindřich Hořejší who in 1921 at the age of thirty-two published his first book of verse, *Hudba na náměstí* (*Music in the Market-Square*). The son of a carpenter, he had struggled through a course as a poor student in pre-war Prague, then had spent five years in Paris. He returned home with a thorough knowledge of modern French literature, and fired by the ideals of the Paris Commune. In Prague he lodged at the house of Karel Teige, where he met many of the young writers, including Wolker, and by reason of his culture and greater age he exerted a considerable influence upon them. His book incorporated many of his wartime poems, including the autobiographical '*Monolog bývalého pěšáka*' ('Monologue of an Ex-infantryman'). In the poem his dreams of distant travel are realized by war, which takes him to Serbia, Russia, and Italy. In all lands he finds the familiar treadmill of life from which he had sought to escape, and through experience he grows to the understanding of his solidarity with all his fellows upon the earth: his brother is the 'enemy' whom he killed in action, and whose face still haunts his memory.[1] In other poems the war itself becomes a symbol of a greater struggle, whose cause is the liberation of mankind. To the poet the city, that triumph of industrial and technical progress, becomes an object of horror and detestation, a vast spider's web in which millions of human flies struggle helplessly amid the strands that trap them. A nest of social injustice and slavery, a pandemonium of bustle and noise, a desert that swallows humanity—such are the guises of the city in Hořejší, above all a stone labyrinth in which man is lost even among the crowd. Through this labyrinth walk young lovers: fortified by their youth and hopes, resolute in their pilgrimage, they step into the future. They are the children of the revolution who, defying the fears and doubts of their elders, walk secure in the knowledge that they are not alone. Hořejší combined two motifs typical of Proletarian poetry; on the one hand, the feeling that the lost individual finds himself at last in the ranks of the proletariat; on the other hand, the contrast between the reality of the present and the dream of the future—a gap that is spanned only by the arch of social revolution.

Similar in theme but different in atmosphere was another book published in the same year. It was *Město v slzách* (*A City in Tears*) by a young poet, who was a member of the Union group and of the *Devětsil*, Jaroslav Seifert. Like Hořejší, Seifert took modern city life as the subject of his verse, and like the older poet he exposed beneath the gay facade of technical civilization the painful struggle for existence on which it was based: the machines that were built to serve man now enslave him: that which was to be his greatest pride and triumph is now

---

[1] Compare Wilfred Owen's poem 'Strange Meeting'.

the instrument of his degradation. The world of the urban proletariat was home to Seifert and he writes of it with assurance and without sentimentality. This assurance lies in the tremendous strength which he feels as one of the masses—a waterfall of human bodies, a spreading sea which covers the earth. As the legions of Egypt pursuing Moses were drowned in the Red Sea, so will those who would withstand the revolution be swallowed by it. Through the poem '*Řeč davu*' ('The Crowd Speaks') in solemn repetition runs the cry, '*Jsme dav*' ('We are the crowd'): the theme is the titanic strength of the marching masses at whose bidding the sun itself would be extinguished if they spat into its face.

Seifert differed from the would-be Proletarians among his bohemian friends in that he was genuinely of working-class background. Whereas Wolker in his poems sought in spirit to enter into the proletarian world, Seifert was eager to escape from its limitations. But his ideas of revolution are rather romantic, and his vision of the promised land of socialism is not unlike the picture of a typical working-class holiday. In style Seifert tried to be simple, achieving his aim by piling expression on expression: aiming to depict the workers' world, he wrote in their language and brought the form of poetry close to that of ordinary speech. Because the cultural background of the masses was basically religious, his poems are drenched in biblical imagery, and a recurring form of expression with him is the prayer. His ethic is that of Communism, but the vehicle of its expression is Christian:

> We do not forgive in the name of love
> the sins of men:
> we firmly avenge in the name of love
> the starving lives,
> the unrighteousness,
> that man, in Thy image created,
> on his brother man has inflicted
> on the earth, in the sky, on the sea.[1]

---

[1] Ve jménu lásky neodpouštíme
spáchaný hřích,
ve jménu lásky tvrdě mstíme
životy hladových
a příkoří,
jež člověk, stvořený k obrazu tvému,
činil bratru svému
na zemi, na nebi, na moři.

The young writers had been casting round for a platform for their views, and this they found temporarily in a so-called Artists' Club, which agreed to produce a new journal, *Orfeus*. In order to improve the chances of the journal's survival contributions were sought and obtained from established writers, including Hora and K. Čapek. When the first number appeared (in 1920) it was clearly dominated by the big names on the one hand, and by the avantgardists on the other. The latter represented the ultra-modernist wing of the Union group, and for effective purposes they were led by a budding art critic Karel Teige. The latter, though never a great creative writer, was a dominant figure in Czech cultural life between the wars. An artist, essayist, and critic of architecture, he was a born leader, and had he devoted himself to any one branch of art, he could have been outstanding: as it was he proved to be a perpetual student and dilettante, a *bon viveur* and the leading theoretician of the whole Czech avantgarde movement. The group around Teige included the young novelist Vladislav Vančura, the poet Jaroslov Seifert, and the artist Adolf Hoffmeister.

The new journal lasted only three issues, and after it was liquidated the hopeful young poets began to look around for a new platform. Meanwhile Teige and the avantgardists had resigned from the Club and founded their own organization, the *Devětsil*, devoted to revolution in art, life, and politics. In a counter-move Wolker and Kalista combined with a more conservative group, headed by a young Moravian critic František Götz, to found a journal which they agreed to call *Host* (*The Guest*). The title of the journal was taken from that of Wolker's first book of poems which was then in preparation.

During 1921-2 the Union group of young writers divided into two rival but friendly camps, the Communist, avantgarde circle of the *Devětsil*, and the moderates whose platform was the journal *Host*. The programme of the latter group was defined in a manifesto, published in the Autumn issue in 1922, which emphasized the ethical and spiritual values which lay behind its socialist humanism. While accepting the need for economic revolution which would end the division separating man from man, it claimed that political revolution in itself was not a programme, and would not improve the human state unless accompanied by a moral revolution. The artistic work of the group was intended to further these ends. The movement was therefore activist and socially engaged, like the Proletarian writers of the *Devětsil*, but unlike them it was not tied to a political party, and was anxious to avoid extremism of any kind.

Among the pioneers of the *Host* group had been Kalista and Wolker, and the former was a signatory of the manifesto. The programme of the group was binding on all its members, and the choice of supporting it or resigning no doubt helped to drive Wolker to a more extreme position. In this situation Wolker resigned from the group and switched his allegiance to the *Devětsil*. His letters reveal that he still had many reservations about the latter, but his ideas had been developing in a more radical way during his stay in Prague, and his personal relationship with Kalista had cooled considerably. At any rate he rapidly became the spokesman for the *Devětsil* on artistic questions, and in a vehement published statement he declared that Proletarian art must be aggressive, non-humanistic, and dogmatic, its only beauty being its social faith and its inner truth.

Wolker's theoretical ideas on art were put into practice in October 1922 when his second book of verse appeared. It was *Těžká hodina* (*The Difficult Hour*), which was to become the classic example, and the swansong, of Proletarian literature. The critical hour of which the title speaks is that of painful transition between childhood and manhood. Between the death of the child's heart and the birth of the man's, between the loss of innocence and the birth of resolution, falls the shadow of disbelief and despair. The resolution is needed to fulfil his vocation, which is nothing less than to make the laws of life conform to the image of his own heart. At the moment when his faith abandons him, he calls for help from the still-life of intimate objects in his room—a letter, a lamp, and a friend's book. All three are associated in his mind with friendship, they are in fact symbols of the lost paradise of harmony —and it is this broken harmony which is the basic motif of the book. Wolker now sees only the poor, the sick and the down-trodden: heroism appears only in the crushed, and the only true reality is found in the broken spirit of the proletariat. It is to the drunks that God chooses to appear, and His glory is proclaimed in the inns and brothels of the city underworld. The function of art in this world appears in the poem '*Slepí muzikanti*' ('The Blind Musicians'). With fiddle and harmonica the two humble players transform the world of the slums into a thing of beauty, and the audience grows new eyes to witness this transformation. But the musicians are, in the end, only blind beggars, and their reward from the audience is disappointing. The guilt is theirs who see suffering and do not help, for their blindness is of the heart, and contrasts with their vision of a better world. The principle of harmony, basic to Wolker, is extended to cover human suffering: as one creature lives by the death of another, so human happiness is won only by the despair of others. A love song begins in traditional style, praising the eyes of the beloved which embrace the whole world: a workman falls to his death from scaffolding before the poet's eyes, and for this she is, in some mystical sense, held to blame by him. Having lost innocence Wolker has found guilt. In '*Setkání*' ('The Meeting') Wolker sits in a café with prostitutes, one of whom is the double of his sweetheart; he sees her face appear below the surface of the water: she has drowned herself for the sake of their happiness. As in his earlier book Wolker repeatedly regroups people and objects into fresh relationships, like coloured glass in a kaleidoscope, and the organizing principle is one of ethical harmony. Amid the mystical fellowship and the total inter-dependence of living things the guilt of one is balanced by the sacrifice of another, just as the happiness of one is purchased only by the misery of another; so that happiness itself becomes a ground for guilt.

In the '*Balada o očích topičových*' ('Ballad of the Stoker's Eyes') which proclaims the immortality of creative work, Wolker combines the theme of transubstantiation with that of sacrifice. Into the furnace of the power-house the stoker feeds not only coal but also his own eyes, and they are transformed into the light that illuminates the homes of others. At the moment of blindness he recognizes and accepts his sacrifice:

> That moment Antonin, the horny stoker, saw
> his five and twenty years beside the furnace door,
> the years in which the knife of flame had cut his eyes,
> and recognizing that a man can ask no more
> than this—to die a man—above the darkness wide,
> above the spreading world, enormously he cried:
>
> 'Comrades of the power-house,
> I am blind—I cannot see.'[1]

---

[1] V tu chvíli Antonín, topič mozolnatý,
poznal těch dvacet pět roků u pece, u lopaty,
v nichž oči mu krájel plamenný nůž,
a poznav, že stačí to muži, by zemřel jak muž,
zakřičel nesmírně nad nocí, nad světem vším:

„Soudruzi, dělníci elektrárenští,
slepý jsem,—nevidím!"

c

Yet in sacrificing himself he has sacrificed his wife and child, and as she
sobs, the darkness of her sorrow is pierced by the electric rays of the
light that her husband gave to all men by his work:

And yet above the dark, the dark of blindness, hangs
a lamp of radiant light—no radiant lamp but eyes:
the eyes are yours that gave to all the world their sight,
to see most clearly, and never dim their light.
Exalted, stoker, though your tortured body die,
you gaze down on yourself, in blindness as you lie.

The worker is mortal
the work lives on,
the stoker is dying,
the lamp sings on:

'Weep no more,
my love, my wife,
weep no more!'[1]

The stoker who loses his sight, the woman who loses her husband, are
both victims of the social law which demands reciprocal sacrifice so
that life can go on: light is won by darkness; the laughter of one is
bought by the tears of another. Thus are men united in a mystical
fellowship of work and suffering, for the world of men is a community
of creators—those who by their labour feed life into the world so that
they may, in return, draw life from it.

In the '*Balada o nenarozeném dítěti*' ('Ballad of the Unborn Child')
a child is conceived, but the lovers decide they are too poor to allow it to

---

[1] však nad černou slepotou veselá lampa visí,
to není veselá lampa,—to jsou oči čísi,
to oči jsou tvoje, jež celému světu se daly,
aby tak nejjasněji viděly a nikdy neumíraly,
to jsi ty, topiči, vyrostlý nad těla zmučené střepy,
který se na sebe díváš, ač sám ležíš slepý.

Dělník je smrtelný,
práce je živá,
Antonín umírá,
žárovka zpívá:

Ženo má,—ženo má,
neplač!

be born. The conception of the child is described in language recalling the sacrament:

> Love is man and wife,
> love is bread and knife.
> My love, I cut the bread
> and from the wound a stream
> has stained my hands to red.[1]

The warmth and passion of the conception is contrasted with the icy carbolic atmosphere of the abortionist's surgery. As the lover stands at the door in the agony of waiting during the operation, he takes upon himself the guilt for what has happened. When the girl steps from the surgery, she is drained of all life, a walking grave, a wound, that the dead hands of a child had caressed. The relationship of the lovers is destroyed with the embryo, and yet they had committed no crime against the natural law which drew them together. The code of morals established by the social order is in direct conflict with the natural code, and poverty has forced upon the lovers a new and terrible ethic, to kill their own love. The individuals, tortured by guilt, are not to blame: the flaw lies in the system that demands a senseless sacrifice which, unlike that of the stoker, produces no answering good. The stoker sacrificed himself to generations yet unborn: the lovers sacrifice the unborn to the futility of the social system.

If the first two ballads deal allegorically with the philosophy of labour and the social implications of human conduct, the third ballad, '*Balada o snu*' ('Ballad of a Dream'), deals with revolution itself. A young worker, Jan, is haunted by the dream of a better life, and the dream gets always in the way of action to realize it. At last he decides to kill the dream—even beauty and imagination must be sacrified to the social goal—and the poem ends in a tremendous panorama of revolt, as the myriad hosts of workers pour into the streets.

Wolker's poems reflect a constant search for a lost harmony, and this he finds—or tries to find—in identification with the working masses,

---

[1] Láska je žena a muž,
láska je chleba a nůž.
Rozřízl jsem tě, milá má,
krev teče mýma rukama
z pecnu bílého.

the only true reality, or the most real reality, as he himself described it. As salvation lay in solidarity with one's fellows, so true damnation lay in isolation from them, and Wolker frequently experiments with this motif. In a later poem, '*Balada o námořníku*' ('Ballad of a Sailor'), which was inspired by Coleridge's 'Ancient Mariner', a sailor expiates his guilt by exile from his kind in a lighthouse, and, as token of his expiation, watching the sea by his side stands God, the unseen Guest of Wolker's first book.

Těžká hodina marked the peak of Czech Proletarian writing, but the movement itself was near its end. Its champion was Wolker himself, and after his break with Götz and the *Host* group, he had placed all his hopes in the *Devětsil*, and had practically identified the movement with its members. But the *Devětsil* stood for revolution in art as well as in politics, and Wolker's revival of the folk ballad was too conservative for their taste. Members of the group were far from united about the whole principle of using poetry as a political weapon, and were inclined to regard the employment of creative literature in this way as a degradation of art itself. When Wolker first put forward in detailed form the programme of Proletarian art, at an evening organized by the journal *Var*, it was a member of the *Devětsil* and a friend of Wolker who rose to attack it. The man was Vítězslav Nezval, whose name was to dominate Czech avantgarde art for twenty years, and he refused to accept the thesis that art had any other function than to be itself. It was the first shot in a campaign that was to end in the total triumph of the avantgarde over the socially activist form of art. Within the *Devětsil* a sharp blow to Wolker's cause was delivered by Karel Teige who, after enthusiastically supporting Wolker's stand on Proletarian art, with equal enthusiasm switched to the opposition. But the end of the phase was precipitated in fact by the misfortunes of Wolker himself. His letters from the winter of 1922 are full of doubts and gloomy thoughts. As a writer he felt that he had shot his bolt, and after seeing the latest work of the *Devětsil* he feared that the very term Proletarian art had become a bad joke. He thought of founding a new journal, but felt he had lost nearly all his friends, and feared to be let down again. Teige wrote and invited him to contribute to a new journal *Disk*, but Wolker declined, adding that he found it difficult to co-operate in conditions of mutual distrust. In a letter he mentions his increasing aversion to modern trends in art, and describes his current writing as close to Decadence. After considerable hesitation he made a final break with the *Devětsil* and sent in his resignation. Wolker had suffered from repeated ill-health in Prague, and in April of 1923 an X-ray revealed tuberculosis: he was sent to a sanatorium in Slovakia where he produced a new cycle of realist poems drawn from hospital life. In October his recovery was halted by a relapse and his correspondence shows increasing despair. He wrote his own epitaph and sent it to Hora, who declined to publish it, thinking that Wolker's enemies would regard it as a pose. He died in January before reaching the age of twenty-four.

Through the short years of Wolker's productive life the atmosphere of his poetry had shifted imperceptibly from the naive world of childhood to the complex world of human suffering, from a simple pattern of idyllic harmony to a tense equilibrium of human relationships in which the happiness of one member is inevitably purchased by the sacrifice of another. Writing at a time when political faith could still be utopian, he sought personal freedom by service to the collective spirit, and fulfilment by submerging his own individualism within the crowd. Convinced that art was a social form and a proper instrument of social development, he offered his poetry to its service and sought to become the mouthpiece of the mass revolutionary spirit. The need to keep his work comprehensible to the masses ruled out experimentation of form, and in formal matters he made no original contribution to Czech poetics. His strength lay rather in his gift of imagination and composition, whereby he was enabled to excel in the art of metamorphosis of people and objects, and in the transformation of the everyday into the miraculous, rather in the fashion of the fairy tale. Expressionism had taught him the power of simplicity and naturalism in art, and perhaps it was this above all that saved his work from the great danger of the Proletkult movement—the danger of art being swamped by ideology. Yet Wolker paid for his social principles: for in the effort to become the mouthpiece of a reformist cause the personal poet of *Host do domu* rejected the personal factor in his own work, and denying himself the natural role of the lyric poet, he chose to tread the hard and thankless path of the social prophet. By his later disillusion Wolker revealed his awareness of how unfit he felt himself to be for such a task; for the guide who would lead others must himself be without doubts or compunction. It is given to few men to combine the role of poet and prophet, but it is typical of Czech early postwar literature, when all values were in question and all roads seemed open, that there should be a loss of balance and perspective, so that young writers failed to see the essential limitations of the literary craft. The friends who deserted Wolker, as he thought, had in fact realized that a poet can never be more than a poet, and that art can have no greater fidelity than to itself. And yet in one sense Wolker succeeded beyond his dreams. If he lost the adherence of the artists, he gained the ear of the masses, and his work lives on in the hosts of his admirers. But the road along which he seemed to be leading Czech poetry turned out to be a blind alley, and he had no successors. During the last year of Wolker's life and in his absence from Prague, new work had been appearing, and a new programme had been formulated, which pointed in an entirely different direction and was to produce the most striking and original work in modern Czech poetry.

3

POETISM

AMONG Wolker's friends in Prague had been a young student, Vítězslav Nezval, a member of the *Devětsil* group, and the first to speak out against Proletarian art. Though the two budding poets were both ardent revolutionaries, by comparison with Nezval, Wolker appeared at times almost a conservative. Whereas the latter had brought to the turbulent group a salutary touch of earnestness and discipline, Nezval surpassed all in his gay and impudent disrespect for convention, both in life and art. While Wolker felt himself to be the voice of collective feelings, Nezval was essentially an individualist. To other members of the group revolution was a programme for social action and a theme of art: to Nezval revolution was almost a way of life, an instinctive expression of his unruly nature which fled from conformity and preferred the outrageous to the conventional.

Nezval's poems document the secret life of his imagination, and from his own confessions we can trace the steps which led him to poetry. Among his most vivid early impressions was the feeling of terror induced by dreams, a terror lingering on when its cause had been forgotten with the dream. It was a feeling which could have no logical exposition nor be subjected to rational analysis, since the terror could not be related to any remembered experience: its compelling urgency existed, as it were, in the void, and could be rationalized within no context of incident. At first the young Nezval believed that such emotion, divorced from visualized action or logic, could adequately be expressed only through the medium of music; and it was when he became dissatisfied with the technical level of his own musical attainments that he turned to verse, as to a new field of improvization in patterns of sound. In the poetry of the Czech Decadents Nezval found that atmosphere of suggestive uncertainty, that exploration of the dream world, which touched a familiar chord within himself; and he began to write verse in the style of Machar and Dyk. While still in his teens he shook himself free of his models and yielded himself to that remarkable fantasy which was his greatest gift. It was then that Nezval first read Karel Čapek's anthology of modern French poetry. Like a revelation were spread before the young poet accomplished products of a literary style which accorded with his own barely glimpsed aims—the stream of consciousness, and liberation from logical continuity in the work of Apollinaire; and the prose poems of Rimbaud, linking the reader with crystallized fragments from the forgotten mass of the poet's childhood impressions. It was the example of the French poets which taught Nezval to delve for inspiration in the hidden store of his forgotten past. In a way later made famous by the Surrealists he thus learned to suspend the censorship of his own conscious mind, and to write according to no preconceived plan but in accordance with the promptings of his subconscious mind. So Nezval was led to the unrelenting pursuit of spontaneity in composition—a spontaneity that ignored traditional patterns of logic or experience. While his friends were writing the socially committed literature of the Proletarian phase, Nezval went his own way, and produced that distinctive cycle of poems which he published in 1922 under the title of *Most* (*The Bridge*).

Among his most vivid impressions of Prague was the night-time view down the river, in which bridge after bridge appeared as a necklace of lights reflected in the moving water. In each bridge he saw a symbol of transit between two unknowns, and, in the title poem of his book, a symbol of human life. Once the traveller sets foot upon the bridge he forgets his destination. Lost among his petrified fellow travellers, he is drawn by the winking light from the cabin of a boat upon the gloomy water: having forgotten his past, he surrenders his future to the moving dream. This motif, the surrender of consciousness to fantasy, dreams, and death, appears elsewhere in the book, often associated with the image of water. There are poems which consist of a stream of unconnected pictures without logical meaning: there are also fairy tales of the subconscious mind, startling, paradoxical, and of a very queer charm, in which normal categories of time are reversed, and the only reality is the dream. Many of the poems are in unrhymed free verse, but where metrical regularity and rhyme appear, they are used with telling effect. An example is the poem '*Zasnění*' ('Brief Dream'), with its nightmarish still-life of moonlight on a cracked mirror; a rocking cradle; a clock striking across water; dying flowers; and a dreaming child riding towards death on a ghostly horse.

It is natural that a poet brought up on the literature of Decadence should flirt with the gloomy attraction of death; Nezval's efforts in this regard are surprising for their sophistication. The poem '*Smrt*' ('Death') has its beginning in the future, and its setting in the poet's grave. The paradise of the future is that which was often glimpsed in his past life, scenes from which flit past in reverse order until the very first moment of recollected childhood appears. He is three years old, and watches the figure of his father moving stealthily across the yard of his home: the figure stops, and the child holds his breath in unbearable suspense. There is an explosion, as his father shoots a rat, and in the flash of that moment all secrets are suddenly revealed. The child's heart stops. He dies, bringing the wheel full circle; he has crossed the bridge of life again, but in reverse direction.

It was evident from his first book that Nezval's view of poetry was quite different from that of Wolker and his friends. He was from the beginning suspicious of verse orientated to ideological issues, and was prepared to debate the question with the *Devětsil*. In April of 1922 he attended a student meeting at which Seifert read a paper entitled 'The New Proletarian Art'; and Nezval, who had gone to criticize, was surprised and impressed by the novelty of the approach. The speaker stressed that proletarian culture existed in a bourgeois world, and writers should not confuse the demands of some future socialist society with the present. To have any effect, art must operate through media acceptable to the common man, who sought not propaganda or uplift but entertainment. The artist and his public, now cruelly divorced, could be brought together again only by destroying the barrier between highbrow and lowbrow art. The man in the street found recreation in the epics of cowboy films, sensational American serials, football, the circus, and the music hall. It was from these that revolutionary art must begin—Jules Verne and Buffalo Bill were closer to the heart of the proletariat than the Communist Manifesto. Even as the skilful writer could win the interest and train the taste of a child by the fantasy of the fairy tale, so must the artist bridge the gulf to his public by works no less exotic and fantastic than those of Verne, but linked to the lives, dreams and aspirations of the common man.

Nezval was delighted with this approach, which accorded so closely with his own ideas, and the very next day he sought out Teige to express his support for the programme. At their first meeting Nezval began to recite an unpublished poem which could have been specially written to fulfill the theoretical requirements of the lecture. It was '*Podivuhodný kouzelník*' ('The Amazing Magician'), and at the request of both Teige and Seifert the *Devětsil* included it in a volume of their work which they published in the same year (1922).

The poem is set partly in the real world, partly in that of dreams: its action moves between the categories of time and of wish-fulfillment. Its beginning finds the poet wandering from the lights of the town to the darkness of his own imagination:

> One evening I walked by the river
> in the gloom like a shimmering mirage,
> following the lead of the street-lamps
> that twisted through alleys
> opened like jaws of a beast.
> Night came rushing upon me
> in the chiming of clocks, a piano
> poignantly echoing over the water.[1]

Through the darkness looms a convent, apparently a symbol of the unawakened, ascetic spirit of the Czech people, and of a social order which is death to creative art. Here the poet is witness to the miracle of a virgin birth, the coming of a magician-poet who is the hero of this strange epic. In this figure can be recognized the poet-liberator of Wolker's conception, but instead of the dedicated martyr it is a figure more appropriate to the circus or the film fantasy—an illusionist whose only stable characteristic is instability. Nezval reveals, in his pedigree, the sources of the magician's power. Below him whole layers of reality stretch down to the centre of the earth: beneath the life of logic and the senses at the surface lie memories and forgotten impressions which live out their own secret life, and continually force their way upwards to appear above ground as dreams and hallucinations. They are terrifying and incomprehensible to logical minds, which keep thrusting them back below the surface; but full of power to the poet, who retains the insight of the savage or of the child. At the centre of this seething mass bubbles

---

[1] Jednoho večera procházeje se podél nábřeží
jež bylo ponuré a světélkující jak fatamorgána
dal jsem se vésti lucernami
jež točily se v průjezdech
rozevřených na způsob zvířecí tlamy
a noc chvatem se přibližovala
vcházejíc do úderů hodin a do piana
jež smutně se rozléhalo až na druhém konci řeky

a fountain which restlessly pushes upwards, forever striving to burst through the crust of earth into the light of day, and with every thrust beating out a song of creation.

This Freudian allegory is merely an introduction to the magician's fantastic adventures, as he seeks relief from the restricting feelings of terror and guilt which pursue him. His childhood is haunted by the vision of a cat staring through a window, the memory of a dead playmate, his relationship with his mother, and an unattainable vista of romance in the form of a mysterious lady of the lake. To escape memories he plunges into action, rushing from Madrid to London, from Paris to Petrograd. Hoping to find release through revolution, he raises the flag of revolt and leads the cheering crowds to the barricades. But social revolution is not the key which can free him. Reliving the terrible vision of the cat he awakes with a cry, and finds the lady of the lake, whom he mistakes for his mother. By her he is relieved at last of guilt, and returns to the world of childhood experience. So his adventures continue, as he seeks to liberate others by his powers, organizing the regiments of the dead against death. At last the magician himself is dissolved again to his primal atoms: dying, he returns to the stream of life. From the moon he sees upon his own petrified corpse the lady of the lake crouching in the form of a tigress as the now liberated fountain spurts up into the air. At last the meaning of the poem's prelude becomes clear:

> New is the culture you dream of, and new variations I sing you,
> tigress-decked fountain that rises over the grave of that dead child.
> Loudly rang out the post-horn. On raced the horse to the meadows
> charming to tears the stars. Come march to the rainbow I sing you![1]

'The Amazing Magician' was a startling realization of the ideas still being worked out by the theoreticians of the *Devětsil*, combining as it did the themes of fantasy with revolution—revolution viewed not merely as a change in the social order, but as a liberation of the human spirit. By a strange transformation the call to the barricades, which had been for Wolker a summons to sacrifice, had now become a signal for

---

[1] O nové kultuře sníš a já nově ti v proměnách zpívám
fontáno s tygřicí jež jsi náhrobkem tohoto děcka
Troubil postilion a koníci běželi k nivám
rozplakat oči hvězd Má píseň je duhou s ní kráčej

happy release from inhibitions, a symbol not of struggle and suffering but of gaiety and carnival. If art was to Wolker a weapon in the social struggle, to Nezval the social struggle was a theme of art. The volume in which Nezval's poem appeared bore witness to the diversity of the *Devětsil's* interests. Besides verses contributed by Wolker and Seifert were poems of Cocteau and Goll, illustrations of Charlie Chaplin and Douglas Fairbanks, a discourse on the pleasures of the 'electric century', and articles by Ilya Ehrenburg and K. Teige. The latter pleaded for art based on the modern beauties of the machine age. The film was today as pregnant with cultural possibilities as the printing press had been at the time of the renaissance: it was on the techniques of the film that modern poetry should base itself. The new art was the expression of revolution in a whole living style: *the new art would in fact cease to be art* in the traditional sense.

It is clear that the views of Teige and his friends were based on the current doctrines of constructivism and functionalism. One of Teige's main loves was architecture, as a branch of art which was directly concerned with satisfying the material needs of man, and many of his more illuminating comments on literature were in fact inspired by the concept of literary functionalism. As examples of modern art of the machine age were cited the yacht and aeroplane, whose beautiful lines were suited to the practical requirements of life. In the same way, the only true modern poetry was that which was suited to its social function which was certainly not didactic, but emotional and aesthetic—the function of supplying that element of excitement and freedom which the restraints of modern society tended to destroy.

The essence of Teige's complaint against Proletarian poetry was that its view of poetry's function was out of date: verse was no longer a useful weapon in the social struggle, as it had been in the past. There were art forms ready to hand which were much better suited to the task of mass persuasion—the poster or the caricature, for example—and a traditional form like poetry could not compete with them in this area. Once poetry had possessed specific functions, like being a guide to the rhythm of work, but such functions had long since been taken from it, and in the literary field the task of political education was better carried out by journalism. Poetry had in fact become a luxury product, retaining its emotional function as a safety valve for emotions not permitted their due outlet by sophisticated society: unlike journalism, poetry could express man's inner life, his private world of magic, violence, heroism, and dreams. Those who tried to use poetry as a medium of mass persuasion were deceiving only themselves: writers like Nezval and Seifert were more realistic in their attitude, and their experiments in form and theme were designed to attune poetry to the modern world, and to extract from it what new sensations it would yield. In 1923 Seifert published a new book of verse '*Samá láska* (*Nothing but Love*)' which marked a transition in his work. In one poem he combines the theme of love and revolution—the meeting place of the lovers is at the barricades. A lullaby describes the day of revolt, of waving banners, a shot, and a body that falls within the crowd. The march of the rebels fades into the rocking of the cradle and the mother's quiet singing, in a restrained ending like the final fadeout in a film. The book is marked by a curious dichotomy: on the one hand the call to revolt, ascetic endurance, and rejection of the bourgeois world; on the other an increasing appreciation of, and enjoyment of, that very world. In the introductory poem Seifert, in the semi-humorous fashion which became so typical of his style, invoked the modern muse which each evening draws back the curtain from the cinema screen; which guides the hand of the skyscraper designer; which holds the circus clown's hoop and leads the pony on whose head the dancer balances. Poems in the later section of the book exploit the charms of the modern technical world, and summon up visions of waving palms, exotic far-away paradises, sandy shores, and zooming aeroplanes. The seal is set upon the book by its concluding poem '*Všecky krásy světa*' ('All the Beauties of the World'). Seifert's idea of art now excludes the poet who writes of stars and flowers:

> Die with the stars, poet, fade with the flowers!
> No one will miss you at all,
> your art and your glory will vanish for ever
> like posies arranged on a tomb.[1]

As the electric glamour of a modern town outshines the poor flowers, so to Seifert the poet's voice is now superseded by the sound of the aeroplane. The beauty of the world is to be seen today from the top of a skyscraper, and its miracles upon a cinema screen. As the old forms of

---

[1] Básníku, umři s hvězdami, uvadni s květinou,
nezasteskne se už nikomu dnes po tobě,
tvé umění, tvá sláva navždycky zahynou,
neboť jsou podobny květinám na hrobě.

beauty are outshone, the traditional art which enshrined them is dead
and unmourned:

> art is dead: the world lives on without it.[1]

Seifert's light-hearted claim could perhaps be rephrased as 'ART is
dead: long live art.' The avantgardists were keen to eliminate the
distinction between 'high' and 'low' art, as for example by the accept-
ance of new forms like the film: they were also prepared to question the
most fundamental concepts of art and literature. In this they were
undoubtedly influenced by the so-called Dada movement which
reached Prague in the twenties when its momentum was already spent
in France. Born of war and confusion, Dada had attacked all values,
ridiculed all art, science, and philosophy, proclaiming that all ideas were
nonsense but that nihilism was its most acceptable form. The dadaists
held exhibitions in which visitors were forced to enter through a
public lavatory, and were handed hatchets with which to attack the
exhibits. Dadaist poems turned out to be randomly arranged bus
tickets, and were recited to the accompaniment of electric bells: a
dadaist masterpiece was discovered to be a print of the Mona Lisa
embellished with moustaches. They presented theatre sketches with
such titles as 'The Interloping Navel' or 'The Anti-pyrine'. Dada
specialized in sick jokes and zany humour. It sought to debunk everything; its only weapon was ridicule and its only gospel laughter.

In the Proletarian phase of Czech literature the social responsibility
of art had been overweighted, and it was natural that the swing away
from it should tend towards the opposite extreme—towards the cult of
mischievousness and irresponsibility. In addition, a wave of increasing
disillusion among Czech intellectuals had by 1924 created the kind of
atmosphere suited to dadaist scepticism,[2] with its total rejection of the

---

[1] umění je mrtvo, svět žije bez něho

[2] See, for example, the comments of Bruce Lockhart in his book *Retreat from Glory*:
'In Russia I had witnessed a proletarian revolution. It had been everything that
individual likes and dislikes may choose to call it. But it had been on the grand
scale. It had not been petty. Here I was assisting in a petit-bourgeois revolution
with all the pretentiousness and some of the ridiculousness inseparable from every
petit-bourgeois revolution. . . . Everywhere speculation and self-seeking were
rampant, and in the new states the spectacle of honest peasants converting themselves as rapidly as possible into dishonest bourgeois was nauseating. Individual

'establishment', and its despair of any rational solution to social problems. Above all, Dada reminded the young Czech writers that art was
something to be enjoyed. Where there was nothing else left, there was
at least laughter, and where there was laughter, there was hope.
The influence of Dada can be seen in a piece written by Nezval, and
entitled *Depeše na kolečkách* (*Telegrams on Wheels*). It was staged as
vaudeville, and featured a prologue in which the audience swarm on to
the stage. The manager tries to chivy them away, declaring that the
stage is reserved for Artists: the audience shout him down; they will all
take part. The villains of the piece are crooked businessmen, who discover that ridicule is the one weapon against which they are powerless:
they shoot themselves in despair, and the case of revolution is saved by
laughter.

In the newly founded journal *Disk* Nezval published a long poem
ABC, which consisted of an inconsequential string of verses, each
based on a letter of the alphabet. Within each verse the only connecting
link is the loose association of ideas, often inspired by the odd rhymes,
sometimes by the typographical form of the letters. Wolker and the
others had used the stream of consciousness technique in poetic composition with telling effect: by Nezval it was used with such talented
effrontery that the reader was left wondering whether he was reading
subtle intellectual gymnastics or just nonsense. Over such impudent
jingles the orthodox critics of the older generation might well explode,
and earnest, committed young writers like Píša could shake their
heads in bewildered disapproval. It was Nezval who came closest in
spirit to the dadaists, and he rapidly established himself as the *enfant
terrible* of modern Czech literature, an irrepressible clown who wrote
like an angel.

Nezval now published a second book entitled, appropriately enough,
Pantomima. The book included an interesting study on the aims and
methods of the new poetry; and the essay was written in the rapid,
compressed, and suggestive fashion of the verse it described. It totally
rejected poetry's traditional adherence to the laws of logic: modern
poetry was attuned to the nerve-wracking pace of modern times, and

---

selfishness vied with national selfishness in a common effort to hold and add to its
gains. Only one law prevailed—brute force, and it was used unsparingly to make
the weak weaker and the strong stronger. The idealists had failed, because they
had not the necessary willpower to translate their ideals into action. We wondered
how long this madness could last, and talked of the inevitability of revolution.'

raced along from idea to idea often connected only by associated sounds, leaping from point to point like an electric spark. How did such poetry appear? as 'A miraculous bird, a parrot on a motor bike. Comic, cute, miraculous. A material object, just like soap, a pearl-handled knife, or an aeroplane'.

The poems in *Pantomima* well illustrated the accompanying theory. Their aim was quite evidently to be amusing: they contained strings of gaily exotic pictures and improbable situations in the style of a fast-moving adventure film. The book resembled a scrap album of inconsequential pieces, closer to the spirit of vaudeville than serious literature. The titles of some of the sections are suggestive: *Family of Harlequins, Parrot on a Motorbike, The Week in Colours, Exotic Love, Rocket, Cocktails.* The book was enlivened with picture poems—combinations of words and illustrations somewhat in the style of the comic strip. There were pieces in which groups of normally associated objects were deliberately confused to effect new and queer associations; and the book contained sharp cameos of clear poetry among zany examples of cultivated nonsense.

Pantomima was an annoying book for the critics because it was by no means certain how much of it was to be taken seriously. It could rightly be objected that, like the problem pictures of modern painting, the poems were too obscure. This obscurity was not confined to the language: a critic of the realist school observed that Nezval's poetry was a sort of projection of himself, an obsession of his own mind, and had no existence whatever outside the latter. His artistic world was based not on experience at the ordinary level, but on the childish fantasy or dream. His world was filled with ghosts and dolls, not with people, and began where the real world finished. The charm of his work lay in the adroit mixture of horror and irony, the primitive and the sophisticated, irrational chaos and elegant frivolity.[1]

The poems of Seifert and Nezval bore the stamp of their very individualistic authors, but the work of both had enough in common to show they sprang from a single genre. In May 1924 Karel Teige published in the journal *Host* an article entitled 'Poetism', which was in fact a manifesto of the new movement. Thus was given to the world a name which was to be a watchword of Czech avantgarde literature for years to come.

---

[1] A. M. Píša in his book *Směry a cíle* (*Directions and Ends*).

In Teige's view the noblest expression of modern art was to be found not in cathedrals or galleries but in the functional products of technical civilization. The art of tomorrow, as already demonstrated by the architecture of today, would shun romanticism and decoration, and its spirit would be akin to that of geometry or science. But though the new living style was to be, at its best, severely logical, it must also cater for the irrational side of man, that side of him which hungered for the bizarre, the fantastic, and the absurd. For six days would man be rational, but on the seventh would he rest from reason. This recreation, or social hygiene, as Teige regarded it, was the function of Poetism, which thereby supplemented Constructivism, being itself its opposite face.

Poetism was not itself art, but a style of living, an attitude, and a form of behaviour. It was favourable to the growth of an art which was playful, unheroic, unphilosophical, mischievous, and fantastic: it throve in an atmosphere of gaiety and fun, and aimed to draw the attention of its audience from the gloom of factory and tenement to the bright lights of man-made amusement. 'Poetism seeks to turn life into a magnificent entertainment, an eccentric carnival, a harlequinade of feeling and imagination, an intoxicating film track, a marvellous kaleidoscope. Its muses are kindly, gentle and smiling, its glances are as fascinating and inscrutable as the glance of lovers.'

Here Teige paused to take a side-swipe at the Proletarians, pointing out that ideological poetry with 'content and action' was really a relic of a medieval practice whereby moral lessons were driven home by memorized verses. Those who approached most nearly to the spirit of modern poetry were not the philosophers of today, but the dancers, acrobats, and comedians—witty, daring, spontaneous, the creators of modern magic. Poetism was not an -ism at all in the ordinary sense: it was a living style which might be termed 'modern epicureanism'. It aimed at the systematic liquidation of traditional artistic genres in order to establish the reign of pure poetry, and by the latter was meant poetry in the widest sense, including the poetry of films, of flying, of radio, sport, dancing, and music hall.

When Teige's article was published, work in the poetist style had in fact been appearing in the journals for nearly two years. The manifesto proclaimed the aims of the movement and made explicit the rationale which lay behind it: at the same time it challenged orthodox views of art on the one hand, and the views of ideologically-orientated writers on the other. Predictably the conservative critics received the challenge

D

with sarcasm and contempt, branding the poetists as café idlers playing at revolution, and dubbing them a disgrace to Czech literature. Such outbursts caused Teige and his friends no loss of sleep: their behaviour suggests that they delighted in provoking the wrath of the bourgeois. But the break with the Proletarians was a more serious matter, opening as it did an ugly rift within the ranks of the young radicals. An effort was made to bridge the gap when Teige and Seifert, as representatives of the Prague *Devětsil*, joined the editorial committee of the journal *Host*, the organ of the more conservative socialist group at Brno. But the alliance was short-lived. Teige and Seifert soon resigned, to devote their efforts to a new journal *Pásmo* (*Film-strip*), dedicated to avant-garde literature. In this journal they published their conviction that only the left wing of their generation, represented by the *Devětsil*, could claim to be genuinely modern in spirit, and that it was pointless to try to work outside the framework of their own group.

As far as Proletarian poetry was concerned, its momentum was spent; yet in his death Wolker was more powerful than in his lifetime. The popularity of his verse was spreading fast, even among the very people whom he had denounced as his class enemies. For the young avantgardists who prided themselves on their uncompromisingly revolutionary stance, it was annoying to see their former associate adopted as a pet of the bourgeois, and held up to them as a good example. It had been hard to find that to them as radicals the doors of opportunity were closed: but it was harder still to find that they could be flung open and lead no further than a middle-class drawing-room. It seemed ironical that once he was safely dead even a dedicated Communist writer could be adopted by the reactionaries who were still ridiculing the work of his old friends, and to the avantgardists it appeared that the new cult of Wolker was becoming the largest single obstacle in their path. Their reaction came in a brief, unsigned announcement published in the journal *Pásmo*: it was headed ENOUGH OF WOLKER.

He was scarcely dead when he became 'the greatest poet of his generation' .... It is announced *ex cathedra* that Wolker was the beginning and the end of poetry. Yes, he was the alpha and omega, but only of one branch: and poetry today flows on in a different direction. ENOUGH OF WOLKER! This cry is dictated by honesty towards his work. If he could speak, he too would raise his voice against the piling up of sentimental superlatives. ... A poet of the class struggle has been converted into a national poet: his proletarian

fierceness is forgiven him on account of his artistic lack of enterprise. . . .
Wolker wrote simply and naively of the new humanity; that is why we loved
him. But he created no new form. It is immediately after him that new and
great art begins.

This defiant proclamation gave offence not only to the bourgeois
critics against whom it was aimed, but also to many of Wolker's friends
among the radicals. A typical reaction was that of the *Host* group, who
published a quick reply. They objected that it was stupid to complain
that Wolker had been converted from a revolutionary into a national
poet: his work had merely been assimilated into the national tradition.
It was rash of the poetists to claim that the future necessarily belonged
to their own branch of fantasy: another swing of the pendulum might
still restore logic to art. The poetists themselves had abandoned Proletarian art, which they once supported, and now had the impudence to
label others as bourgeois, whereas in actual fact it was difficult to
imagine a more typically bourgeois form of art than poetism itself.
     Even more bitter were the comments of those who clung to the
Proletarian conception of socially committed literature, and regarded
the poetists as deserters from the true path of Communist art. The
avantgardists were in particular a sore disappointment to S. K.
Neumann, and in his reaction to their excesses he gradually moved into
a more extreme position. From 1922 he edited the journal of the Czech
Proletkult movement, whose views closely corresponded to the organization of the same name in the U.S.S.R. The basic conception of
this school of thought was that, since every ruling class creates its own
culture, the proletariat itself, during its transition into a classless
society, would create its own proletarian culture. As examples of this
were cited the local factory newspapers in Russia, entirely written by
the workers themselves.
     In the U.S.S.R., however, it soon became clear that the work of
the factory poets, though of great historical interest, was artistically
insignificant: where they began to compete seriously on a cultural level
the Russian proletarian writers at once turned for inspiration to bourgeois traditions. The idea of a pure proletarian culture in fact turned
out to be a delusion, and the Czech Communist writers who had hoped
for so much from it found themselves at a dead end. In 1923 Neumann
wrote: 'Our artists' search for proletarian art was bound to finish in a
parting of the ways—either towards the proletariat or else towards art.
They were bound to reach the conclusion that man cannot serve two

masters, especially when they are so different, and essentially opposed masters. The art of today remains after all the offshoot of bourgeois culture.'

By 1924 the Czech journal *Proletkult* had ceased to appear, and its editor, disappointed with the course of events, returned to the isolation of his youth, devoting his efforts to the writing of lyric poetry. The hoped-for unity of the post-war literary radicals was finally at an end, and the poetists were left in command of a field already littered with outmoded slogans and discarded manifestos.

4

THE END OF THE CARNIVAL

THE victory of the poetists over the school of socially engaged art seemed to the young bohemians a triumph for modernism. At the same time it represented, perhaps to a greater extent than they realized, a reversal to the main stream of Czech literary tradition. It has been said that Czech literature, like the national character, is without demons: its predominant characteristics have more commonly been stoicism, irony, and scepticism than heroism or pathos. Some of the traditional qualities are to be found in the poems of Wolker, yet his portrayal of the heroic worker was in some way alien to a tradition which held nothing sacred and distrusted everything monumental. Thus the clowning of Nezval, and the rejection by Teige of Art with a capital A, appealed to something very real in Czech literary taste. At the same time the loss of interest in the social themes of art was characteristic of a change in the political atmosphere. The tide of revolution which had swept Europe in the immediate aftermath of the war had receded, and with the stabilization of the old order in the West had come from Russia news of reduced revolutionary fervour and the less exciting tasks of the New Economic Plan. As the Proletarian poets had put their greatest concentration of effort into realistic, social themes, so in the succeeding period the trend was back to individualist art and an emphasis on method and form rather than on content. This is not to say that the dramatic phase of Czech writing typified by Wolker passed away without a trace. Young poets like A.M. Píša went on writing in his style and under his influence for some years. The theme of man's creative nobility of spirit was continued not only by the successors to the Proletarians but also by a new wave of Catholic writers, of whom perhaps the most distinguished was J. Durych. Nevertheless during the second half of the twenties it was the poetists who in retrospect appear as most characteristic of their time, influencing as they did even writers outside their own circle and style.

The young writers were still indefatigably in search of a journal which

43

would act as a platform for their work, and for a time they found it in the periodical *Pásmo*, edited not in Prague but in the Moravian city of Brno. The cosmopolitan aspirations of the Czech avantgardists were emphasized by the layout of this journal, with headlines in French, German, English, and Italian. The range of coverage also emphasized the desire to widen enormously the scope of art. In its first issue *Pásmo* had rather pretentiously included in its table of contents 'Modern prose, poems, marxism, technology, the film and theatre, sport, architecture, the popularization of civic culture, the reproduction of modern pictures and sculpture, photography from five continents, urbanism, constructivism and poetism, the aesthetics of the machine.' The journal was enlivened by the originality and in some cases by the charming idiocy of some of its contributions. A typical example in the first issue was a poetist contribution entitled 'Alcohol and a rose' by a promising young painter J. Štyrský, later to become famous as a surrealist artist. Some of the poems were futuristic in design, relying on typographical arrangements and incorporating mathematical symbols, oddly arranged lines, shapes and blocks: in some cases the poems were evidently intended merely for optical effect, and only a few words appeared among the illustrations. These experiments were in effect an attempt to introduce into poetry the techniques of the poster or the film, and at their most successful they foreshadowed a development not towards new forms of literature but rather towards the problem pictures of modern painting and photo-montage.

In 1925 Seifert published his third collection of verse, entitled *Na vlnách T.S.F.* (*On Waves of Radio*). In form and method the book was completely under the influence of the poetist school. In sharp contrast to the earnestness of the past literary phase, the style was light, ironical, and sentimental. Life, as it appeared in Seifert's poems, had shed all devotion to lost causes and unattainable absolutes: it was a dialogue between people uncommitted to the salvation of the world, a game of tennis in which the stakes were trivial and the rules agreed, a modern carnival signifying nothing but itself, a parlour game featuring the witty gesture and the amusing paradox. When Seifert republished the book in later years, he renamed it *Svatební cesta* (*The Honeymoon*), a title which evokes two themes typical of poetism. The honeymoon is that of the poet freshly in love with life, exploring its attractions with a newly awakened ardour, finding everywhere features that are new, strange, and enchanting. But the honeymoon is also a *journey* with which the poet associated visions of luxury trains, cruise ships, waving palms, and the gleaming lights of Paris boulevards. As, in imagination, he is carried in the sleeping cars past glimpses of exotic scenery, a railway guide becomes a book of verse; the glass of the window which frames the Alps is as brittle and precious as the relationship with his bride, and through it he sees the world with new eyes. Seifert did not attempt to describe this world, but only to suggest it, using the greatest possible economy of language. A series of pictures and impressions was linked by association of thought or sound; the transitions were abrupt, with clues instead of bridges, forcing the reader to supply the connections. A danger of this poetry was that of discontinuity amounting to chaos. In his desire to avoid the trite, he avoided the trodden ways of grammar; not to startle the reader but to speed up the tempo to the pace of a modern film.

> Cigarette smoke
> rises
> tourist in the Alps
> sunshine and abyss . . .
>
> rises to the stars
> drunk in by
> that pillow of boredom
> poetry[1]

The book was a literary kaleidoscope of the modern exotic world of jazz, films, cafés, bars, palm trees, grapes, sunshine and the sea; the last-named being to Seifert the very essence of romance:

> When we yearn for faraway places
> we say:
> Waves of the sea, waves of the sea . . .[2]

---

[1] Dým cigarety
stoupá
turista v Alpách
slunce a hloubka . . .

stoupá až k hvězdám
které pije
poduška nudy
poesie

[2] Když se nám stýská po dálce,
říkáme si:
vlny moře, vlny moře . . .

But if the symbol of romance was the sea, that of modern life was Paris, which Seifert had never seen, but pictured (in his poems) as an earthly paradise of artists, high life, negroes, and apaches. This world remained out of reach, hence romantic, to a poor Czech writer, who accepted its unattainability with an amused resignation in which moral condemnation played no part. In contrast to the resolute stoicism of Wolker, Seifert adopted a position of mild epicureanism. However imperfect the world, moral or ideological reservations should not prevent one enjoying it. Poetry, which for a while Wolker had regarded as the instrument of the prophet, had become a diversion, the art of whiling away precious time, the thin and precarious glass which links our eyes with fleeting pictures of a wider and more colourful world.

The success of the poetists attracted to their style writers whose interests had hitherto lain elsewhere. Among Wolker's friends had been a medical student, Konstantin Biebl, who had been his companion on a holiday in Jugoslavia. Biebl had had more personal experience of the war than any other of the young writers, and Wolker had published as a short story a record of Biebl's wartime adventures in Serbia. His painful experiences in some way set Biebl apart from the avantgardists of his generation who were his natural companions. A born artist with a great gift for words and a highly sensitive ear for music, he lacked both the sardonic resignation of Seifert and the nervous energy of Nezval. In his first two books of verse *Cesta k lidu* (*The Way to the people*) and *Věrný hlas* (*Faithful Voice*) he had followed the Proletarians in his ethical attitudes and didactic approach. The subject-matter of his poetry was his thoughts and personal experiences which had revealed to him moments of heightened living under the threat of extinction.

In 1925 Biebl published, in miniature format, a short collection of poems entitled *Zlom* (*The Break*). The title piece was a long poem with prelude and twelve parts, a dialogue between a soldier and his mother who speak to each other as from different worlds, for the horror of the soldier's memories comes between them. The poem opens at nightfall: the child seeks security from unknown terrors in the lap of his mother, who soothes him with a familiar fairy tale. But the fantasy world of knights, armour, and castles gives way to a grimmer fantasy of guns and dynamite. The style recalls the social ballads of Wolker, interlaced with echoes of the folk song: one part (the tenth) is in fact a bitter parody of a song for children praising the life of a soldier. The other long poem in the book '*Tovarna*' ('The Factory') was of a similar type, a dialogue of two lovers which becomes a stream of imaginative pictures forming a kind of epic of the subconscious, in many places recalling Nezval's 'Amazing Magician'.

But it was in his shorter lyrics that Biebl came nearer to the style of the avantgardists. The poem '*Kraslice*' ('The Painted Egg') opens with a picture of an old woman painting; and her designs provide the starting point for a string of impressions unconnected by logic, impressions which lead from a sarcophagus, across the Nile to burning sands, the pyramids, and the vanished past of Egypt. Elsewhere in the lyrics appear the images familiar in poetist art—waving palm trees, Harlequin and Columbine, olive trees, and the faraway sea—the world of fantasy and the daydream linked by the free play of the imagination and the accidental resemblances of sound. There is something obsessive in Biebl's concentration on an image, and his sound effects are at times intentionally hypnotic:

> Down comes the night, the night of your hair,
> lingering and dreaming.
> Down comes the night, the night of your hair.[1]

When Biebl abandoned the social ballad for the lyric of emotional tension, and allowed the sound pattern, rather than the meaning, to become the organizing principle of his verse, he was following the course set by Nezval and Teige. It is interesting to notice that when a second edition of *Zlom* appeared (in 1929), Biebl had pruned and recast the material. Generally speaking, the second edition had much less a Proletarian flavour than the first. The apparent intention to cut down on anything which did not appeal directly to the senses rather than the intellect shows the self-conscious development of Biebl in the direction of 'pure' poetry, aimed to exploit the magic of sound.

In 1925 Biebl produced another short book of verse *Zloděj z Bagdadu* (*The Thief of Baghdad*), a series of lyrics grouped around a central theme of regret for the death of a lover. The theme lent itself to sentimentality, and in many places recalled the style of the Decadent poets, of whom Biebl, like others of his generation, had been an early addict. In the lyrics he wisely avoided the accents of high tragedy, and the mood of the book is rather one of pleasant nostalgia, expressed in

---

[1] Blíží se noc, tvých vlasů noc
dlouhá a snivá.
Blíží se noc, tvých vlasů noc.

melodious repetitions and enhanced by strange reflections from the
exotic world of Biebl's imagination.

> He walks in cafés through the night
> in search of music and baksheesh,
> his fingers clutching table sides
> in a stupor of hashish.[1]

In the same poem Biebl showed his skill as a miniaturist, ringing the
changes on three adjectives which form the rhyming pattern in the
Czech original, and whose associations of sweetness, love, life, and
death are evoked in a very economical way:

> A sugar cube in black coffee,
> your sweet eyes, sweet lips,
> your white corpse in black earth,
> black earth—sweet corpse.[2]

Biebl shared the common fault of the poetists, in that his obsession
with the sound of words and the associations which they evoked in himself led him at times into infantile rhyming or into incomprehensibility.
Yet he was in general more cautious and self-conscious than Nezval,
and his sensitive ear and imagination enabled him to turn out delicate
and melodious lyrics unencumbered with the decoration or the clowning to be found in much poetist verse. This was written by and for
young people; and a part of its attraction lay in its cult of modernity,
its rejection of bookishness, and its contempt for the inhibitions imposed by tradition. The poetists regarded the disapproval of the older
generation as entirely natural and rather amusing: a much more serious
challenge to their literary position came in fact from a writer and critic

---

[1] Chodívá v noci po kavárnách
za hudbou a bakšišem,
stolů se chytá po stranách,
omámený hašišem.

[2] Kostka cukru v kávě černé,
tvé oči sladké a tvé rty sladké,
tvé bílé tělo v hlíně černé,
v hlíně černé tělo sladké.

who lay between the generations. Although older than the avant-gardists Hora was led by his instincts to their support: but he never shared their iconoclasm, and he was set apart from them by a certain seriousness and restraint, a faith in the continuity of art and a respect for the past which was foreign to the poetists, at least in their early stages. Hora himself was dismayed at the swift demise of Proletarian poetry from which he had hoped for so much, and in which he had played so distinguished a part. He was too wise to press on in a course which literary taste had outdated, but the light-hearted and irresponsible artistic attitudes of the avantgardists filled him with misgivings.

Their poetry is untragic and anti-tragic, like the public opinion of today. The more wretched is our position, the more chaotic its prospects, the more passionate is the longing for the dance, for intoxication. It is the reaction to the tragedy of the Great War, which froze us to the bone—the reaction to revolutionary hopes whose fulfillment is late coming . . . The feeling of our time is not for suffering: it wants to sing, even on the brink of the abyss, and it is not surprising that young poets also want to sing, above all, to celebrate. The wonders of technical civilization join hands with the horrors of political and economic disintegration in the poetry of our trusting Nezvals and Seiferts to form a remarkable idyll. And in the end what else are their ostentatiously advertised programmes, announcing a literature which aims not to be literature . . . except a passionate longing for a happiness which the world lacks, a happiness which some have irrevocably lost and others have not yet found. It is a different question whether this poetry, anti-tragic and consciously, deliberately, stripped of ideology to the stage of childish instinct, can have enough life in it ever to be a real driving force . . . to be anything but light reading to soothe us into an enchanted dream. May not these young poets, setting themselves against thinking in verse, forget to think at all?[1].

In 1925 Hora himself published a new book of verse, *Italie*, which marks the beginning of a new phase in his work. Having abandoned with regret the path of socially committed literature, he yet held aloof from the pyrotechnics of the poetists. The central theme of the book was the poet's impressions on a visit to Italy made in July 1924. It is interesting to note how he treated the theme of travel and exotic scenery, so beloved of the avantgardists. In reading the book one cannot but recall what Italy and the classical lands have meant to the Romantic

---

[1] J. Hora writing in the daily newspaper, *Rudé právo* (*Red Rights*), 20 November 1924.

writers of northern Europe for a hundred years—warmth, music, laughter, blue seas, ripening peaches, and lovely smiling girls—the golden days of a lost paradise.

The title poem of *Italie*, points the contrast between the blue skies, the sunlit laurel, the dreaming air of Italy, and the iron network of smoking factories which symbolize the poet's northern home. In Italy he finds again, but strangely transfigured, the Madonna of northern myth and art, no longer the cold, tortured face which he had himself celebrated in his earlier *Dělnická Madona*, but a girl of the South:

> Down the steps of churches to the white towns' streets
> the Virgin Mary walks . . .[1]

As the Madonna of the north had symbolized suffering and death, the girl of the south was a creature of sunshine and life: the very fishes she carries in her basket squirm with the effort to be alive. Behind the image of the Virgin rise the classic, marble features of Capitoline Venus, like a girl who steps down into the street to meet her lover:

> The high noon sun proclaims her slender silhouette . . .[2]

Amid this environment Hora realizes and expresses his own identification with the north; his nature with its nature, and his art with its art. Its characteristics are conceived as a result of the natural environment: from the long, cold winters springs the perennial nostalgia for lost hopes; from the mists, the leaden skies, and the gloomy forests come the doubts, the melancholy, and the Hamlet-like wavering between action and despair, revolution and resignation: from the harsh environment comes unrelaxing vigilance and the vision of a world in which the mind is always conscious of death, and the ear ever alert for the expected cry of distress.

From all this the sunlight of Italy offers an apparent escape— apparent, not real, for it is in Italy that the poet realizes how much his home environment is part of himself. In the poem *Forum Romanum* he feels the relics of past history as a graveyard, silent and deserted: the

---

[1] Po schodech kostelů do ulic bílých měst
ted' sestupuje Panna Maria . . .

[2] Poledne kolmá chválí útlý její bok . . .

march of legions through the arch of Victory led only to the cemetery. The sunlight on the forum accentuates its long shadows: the broken pillars and armless statues rise like a vast heap of futility, marking the aimlessness of history in its march from nothing to nothing. Amid the ruins of the past appears a sign of life—the poppies, which remind Hora of his little daughter at home, and of the temptation to pick them that she would feel. Through the silence of the ruins comes her voice calling —a child amid the very old, the voice of young life amid death.

The contrast between the sunshine of the south and the hard life of the north is a recurrent motif in the book, and everywhere Hora proclaims his allegiance to the latter. In his poems a recurring symbol of the southern lands is the sea, whose wide expanses contrast with the dark alleys of home: but between the eyes of the poet and the water comes the vision of the apple tree in blossom in Bohemia. Hora finds no escape from the tyranny of his social conscience, and the book contains many echoes of his past Proletarian phase. In '*Roma in aeternum*' the ghosts of the past rise before the poet, and see in the present day how unchanged is the scene from that which they remember. In the modern war-machine the consul recognizes his armies; in the downtrodden masses the emperor sees his abject subjects; in the gilded churches and bowing congregations the high priest sees the temples and worshippers of ancient days. Last of all, the prisons of today reveal to Spartacus a glimpse of those who are forever his brothers.

The poetists, in reaction against the social dedication of the Proletarians, had swung to the opposite extreme, ignoring the social utility of art, and treating it as a luxury product or a complex game. It was Hora's achievement in *Italie* to show a middle way. The book represented for him a revival and development of his own lyrical powers: he had learned from the techniques of the poetists, including their use of exotic themes, without following them into their extravagances.

Meantime the gay flag of poetism was still being flourished with undiminished vigour by V. Nezval. His new collection of poems, published in 1926, was entitled *Menší růžová zahrada* (*The Smaller Rosegarden*). It contained not only lyric poems but also two short ballets, in the poetist spirit of widening the scope of verse. Nezval has recorded some of the background to this book.[1] At a somewhat lonely period of

---

[1] Introduction to the second edition of *Most*, pp. 25-6. See also *Z mého života* (*From my Life*), p. 141.

his life in Prague, when he felt that he had temporarily exhausted childhood recollection as the raw material for art, he paid his first visit to the fashionable spa of Marienbad. The wedding-cake architecture and rococo decoration of the place charmed him, and on his return to Prague, his head swirling with stately gavottes and porcelain shepherdesses, he met by accident a lady whose ornamental appearance and cultivated style seemed to the young writer the embodiment of this delightful and lost world. The book is a souvenir of this romantic episode.

Two of the sections in the book *Elegie* (*Elegies*) and *Kostumy a Madrigaly* (*Costumes and Madrigals*) contain lyrics in his new strain, gracious pastorals and gallant minuets infused with ironic sentimentality and the pleasant melancholy that recalls vanished splendour. Some of the poems were of a luxurious and exotic nature, in which a basic theme was used merely to connect a string of fantastic impressions, queer, freakish, paradoxical, and comic. In the poem '*Prodavačka divů*' ('The Girl who Sold Marvels') the central figure attracts colours, names, and associations to herself like a magnet attracting pins:

> There came a boy with tambourine
> and all the planets offered you
> and out you took your fishy eyes
> and with their hellish stone
> you burned away his gentle eyes
> my vendor-girl of mysteries
> with eyes of water nymphs[1]

Many of Nezval's poems resembled a daydream, in so far as they contained a string of self-sustaining images, a sequence connected only by suggestive echoes. On the other hand the book contained some meditative pieces, in which the writer sought to formulate his ideas on art. The poem '*Elegie*' was a rather pretentious example:

---

[1] A přišel chlapec s bubínkem
a nabízel vám všecky planety
a vy jste vyňala své rybí oči
a jejich pekelným kamínkem
jste vypálila jeho něžné oči
má prodavačko divů
s očima mořských žen

One day we shall become the forgotten poets
and other hands will carry on the torch
when we receive a death certificate
and your reward will be a noble harmony
Then we who year by year have borne the flag
and have seen all that man can see
will watch withdrawn the sinking sun . . .[1]

The poem '*Poetika*' was apparently intended, as its title suggests, as an expression of Nezval's philosophy of composition. The features of modern poetry, in his view, are to be speed, change, ingenuity: the poet must learn to submit to the intoxication of the unconscious, to overturn the laws of nature and to exploit the miraculous—not a craftsman, but a magician and an alchemist of words. Nezval affects here to part company with the world of harlequin and pierrot, the carnival world so beloved of the poetists, because together with all its gaiety and colour, it represented nothing but itself, only proclaiming its stylized and theatrical nature. The type of art towards which Nezval appeared to be heading was represented by the most ambitious poem in the book, '*Premier Plan*' ('The Blue-print'). The poem was, in form, a dream. Above the waters of Bohemia a bell rings an alarm that spreads like a rubber band across the furthermost frontiers of the world—a starting point for a poetist romantic travelogue. The issue at stake is written across the sky by sign-writing aeroplanes, the blue-print of the new world—the social dream of Nezval's generation.

'*Premier Plan*' seemed to be the sign of a new stage in the development of the poetists. In reaction to the preceding literary phase they had swung the pendulum too far for their own comfort, and the view of poetry as an elaborate game, to be played by its own rules and with no end outside itself, was already beginning to pall. In fact the first wave of poetism was already receding in 1926, and a more serious note asserted itself in the work of the avantgardists. Critics writing about this phase have said that the mask of poetism began to fall away, revealing

---

[1] Jednou se stanem zapomenutými básníky
někdo jiný převezme náš úkol
dají nám úmrtní list
a zatím naší odměnou bude velkolepá harmonie
My kdož jsme několik roků nesli prapor
a poznali vše co může poznati člověk
budeme kdesi v ústraní pozorovati západy slunce . . .

the human tragedy below; or that the harsh sound of conflict penetrated the wall with which poetism had sought to fence art around. But such emotive metaphors are scarcely necessary to explain the development. The attitudes of the post-war literary generation were affected by the atmosphere of their day. Hostility to a social organization basically unsympathetic to their own ideals had provoked rebellious attitudes and artistic programmes tied to a programme of political revolution. Ideological frustration had contributed to the appeal of poetism by diverting energies to the cause of revolution in art (which seemed to be more readily attainable) rather than in the field of politics, where the writers had found entrenched forces of opposition and bewildering contradictions. The first wave of poetism had meant a withdrawal of art from politics, but not a withdrawal from the world of men: the art of Nezval and Seifert was almost brashly extrovert, and differed in this regard from powerful Catholic writers like Deml or Durych, in whose art not man, but God, was at the centre of the universe, and whose mystical appeal was a call from the labyrinth of this world to the inner paradise of the heart.

The poetists' preoccupation with the man-made world and the life of the imagination led them always back to the theme of conflict—the antithesis between life as it is and life as it might be, which had been basic to Expressionism. Having abandoned the naive idea of resolving the conflict by sweeping changes to redesign society to their own wishes, that is, to overthrow the existing social order by poetry, they accepted the conflict as an actual feature of life, likely to be with them for some time to come. With the existing situation they contrasted their ideas of what life was like in post-revolutionary Russia, and at the same time elaborated their conception of a new enchanted Erewhon. The avantgardists remained consistently socially-orientated in their outlook, and the crude contrast between poetist fantasy and sordid reality provides some explanation for the wild swings between optimism and pessimism which is characteristic of their work. In 1926, industrial smoke begins to obscure the poetist palm trees, and the gay carnival alternates with a masque of death. A sign of the times was Seifert's new collection, *Slavík zpívá špatně* (*Nightingale out of Tune*).

His last book had been inspired by the motif of exotic travel: now the restlessness is undiminished, but it finds an outlet not in romantic daydreams but in vacillation between intoxication and disillusion; extravagance and despair; the honeymoon and the graveyard. Where Seifert before had chosen Paris and the Mediterranean as subjects for poetry,

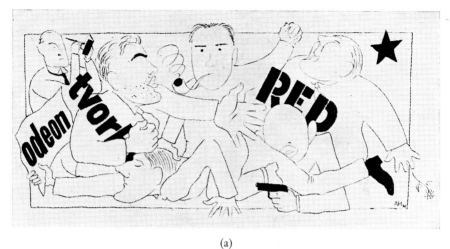

(a)

(b)

1. Contemporary caricatures by A. Hoffmeister:
   (a) 'The Discussion': from left to right, F. X. Šalda, J. Fučik, K. Teige, V. Nezval.
   (b) 'The Avantgarde': K. Teige, V. Nezval, J. Honzl, J. Seifert, J. Voskovec.

2. Cover, designed by J. Štyrský, of Nezval's collection, *Pantomine*, 1924.

now he writes about Verdun. Typical of his new mood is the poem
'*Staré bojiště*' ('Old Battlefield'), depicted as an idiot's delight, a
macabre setting for a dance of death.

> Should we not dance in a cemetery
> between life and death?
> Why not, why not, my dancing girl,
> in an idiots' land?[1]

The dead share their death with the living: we are all dead. The carnival
begins, but the masks are gas-masks; the harlequin's costume is sewn
from the wrappings of corpses: they form the mosaic of death which is
Europe. The motifs of love and luxury, familiar from earlier books, now
reappear in strange guise: the earth is pregnant with corpses; the
bride's dress is of bandages; the cup of wine is a fragment of a grenade;
it is blood that spills from it.

Seifert's intention evidently was to shock and horrify; his paradoxical juxtapositions clamour for attention. In his search for the
startling expression he gave to his poem something of the tone of the
Expressionist paintings so beloved of the early avantgarde. It was a sign
of his maturity that he was cautious in his use of such rhetorical and
verbalist devices. Having absorbed the techniques of poetism, Seifert
used them with studied moderation, avoiding exaggeration in form as
in sentiment. The subjects of his poems ranged over the field of travel,
love, nature; and a whole cycle of poems dealt with the drama of the
new Russia. On all these subjects he assumed a deliberately nonchalant
attitude, avoiding the temptation to strike tragic poses and unfold
apocalyptic visions.

Seifert's book reflected an atmosphere of disenchantment among the
artists of his generation—a group which had lost its certainty, but not
its hope. The first gay interlude of poetism was over, and the mood was
changing to melancholy and disillusion. It was amid this atmosphere
that Hora produced his new book, *Struny ve větru* (*Strings in the
Wind*). The restlessness which inspires the theme of flight and travel
was common to Hora and the poetists: in his new book a dominant

---

[1] Což na hřbitově tančit smí se
mezi životem, mezi smrtí?
Proč ne, proč ne, má tanečnice,
v zemi bláznů?

E

theme is again movement and change, not so much in space as in time. Intrigued by modern theories of natural philosophy, he turned from social to cosmic problems—a most unpromising field for lyric poetry. He did not commit the error of trying to expound philosophical questions in verse, nor do his poems contain any consistent philosophy, but the unrest they often mirror is expressed in metaphysical, not social terms. Hora is especially concerned with the problem of time, and this occupies a whole cycle of verses, grouped together as a section. The title of the book suggests the old romantic idea of an artist as a passive instrument upon which the elements play at their will. In this conception Hora was close to the poetists, for whom the laboratory of art was the world of dreams, the unconscious and irrational land experienced by children and revisited by the drugged, the hypnotized, sleepwalkers, and madmen. The act of creation by the artist is his submission to a power outside himself, and the reality is the current which passes through him, the sound waves that vibrate from his strings. Reality then is a form of energy, felt only as flux, and this feeling Hora expresses by many metaphors, especially from water and air. Time is the soil crumbling under our feet; the present is the imperceivable juncture of the past and the future, the metamorphosis of future into past. Hora is concerned not to be consistent but to inspire awe and terror by bathing the commonplace in cosmic mystery. Yet the cosmos of the poet is a humanized place, and Time appears not only as a tyrant ruthlessly hurrying man into the unknown, but also as a god of sleep and dreams, a secret friend and accomplice of mankind.

> Time, brother of my heart, whose changeless pace
> measures my hours of life in steady number,
> hesitates and recoils before my face,
> lulled into fragrant, flower-like slumber.[1]

The poems in the Time cycle have a skilfully continued atmosphere of hallucinations—the feeling of a sleepwalker stepping on tip-toe for

---

[1] Translated by E. Pargeter:
> Čas, bratr mého srdce, jež jde
> a odměřuje mi hodiny bytí,
> zaváhá, zhroutí se do tváře mé,
> usne a zavoní jak kvítí.

fear of destroying the illusion. The confusion between dream and reality is pointed by Hora's striking use of language:

> across the trodden
> field the sleeper gropes . . .[1]

Like Seifert, he is fond of harsh juxtapositions:

> I hear the twilight ripening[2]

The flux of time is expressed via the modern metaphor of electricity:

> The gales of lights sweep through me,
> sparks crackle from the furry night.
> Behind the wall of dark a hammer beats,
> armies of moments on the march.[3]

Not all the poems in the collection are of the metaphysical type. There are verses based on Hora's impressions of Russia: after the alien relaxation of the south, the gloomy vastness of the northern lands were like home to him. He was by profession a journalist and he had the gifted journalist's eye for the striking touch of language or scenery: a sense of heroism and power is conveyed by his picture of a Russian ploughman silhouetted like a windmill across the steppe. In the personal poems the basic mood is doubt, uncertainty, a paralysis of will—the shadow that falls between the conception and the action:

> I heard someone knock on the door;
> but a voice said to me: Do not open!
> It could not be Spring,
> for Autumn is here.
> It could not be love,
> for she never left.
> And a voice said to me: Do not open!

---

[1] po pošlapané
louce bloudí spáč . . .

[2] Slyším jen šero zrát

[3] Vichřice světel duje mnou,
jiskrami praská noc srstnatá.
Za stěnou tmy bije kladivo,
armády vteřin jdou.

Once again came the knock.
A voice said to me: Go, and open!
Some greeting, maybe, from the distance,
a breath of palms and the sea. . . .[1]

and the conclusion:

Then silence again veiled the doorway;
and I could not but open the door.
The sound of footsteps receding
came echoing back from the street.
It could not be happiness' feet
if she is not within me.
And the air, from her touch, trembled on.[2]

Strings in the Wind may be said to close an interlude in the development of modern Czech poetry. The poetists had contributed much to its development in the way of style, form, and technique, bringing to modern verse fresh vistas of the sub-conscious and the irrational. The first wave of poetism had been characterized not only by fantasy but also by the cult of humour. A contemporary critic remarked that the frustrated young writers found relief from their rebuffs by laughter,

---

[1] Zat'ukal někdo na dveře.
Hlas pravil mi: Neotvírej!
Jaro to nemohlo být,
je podzim již.
Láska to nemohla být,
ta neodešla.
Hlas pravil mi: Neotvírej!

Zat'ukal někdo po druhé.
Hlas pravil mi: Otevři, otevři!
Snad je to pozdrav z daleka,
dech palem a pomoří. . . .

[2] Ticho přikrylo dveře zas.
Musel jsem, musel jsem otevřít.
Na schodech dozníval kroků hlas,
slyšel jsem někoho ze vrat jít.
Štěstí to nemohlo být,
není-li ve mně.
Jen vzduch se ještě po někom třás.

and when other targets failed they laughed at themselves.[1] But in the second half of the twenties the laughter grew rather forced, the jokes rather sick. Characteristically mercurial and extravagant in their attitudes, the young artists were quick to swing from the celebration of life to that of death, from the lyrics of high noon to the poetry of night, conceiving the carnival as over, and its aftermath as a sordid still-life of spilt glasses, faded costumes, and futile make-believe.

---

[1] F. Soldan in his book *Tři generace* (*Three Generations*).

5
POEMS OF THE NIGHT

IN 1927 Nezval published a long poem entitled *Akrobat*—epic in form, lyric in style, and in many ways resembling the earlier 'Amazing Magician'. Like its predecessor the poem is autobiographical; this time its hero appears as a circus tumbler. With bated breath all Europe awaits his arrival, knowing that he will come as a liberator or messiah. Strange stories are told of his fantastic gifts—a ventriloquist, a magician, a joker, a healer of mankind. At last the bizarre figure appears, walking high upon the wire: amid unbearable suspense the crowd follows his progress towards their mysterious salvation. But the tumbler, inadequate for his great task, falls from the wire to his death.

The second part of the work delves back into the past of the poet-liberator. The sequence of impressions runs from the first stirrings of the infant—his first bewildered impulses of erotic brutality—music and loneliness—the aimlessness of his youth and his first experience of death. In each case the train of echoes is traced back to the primary impulse, and from the fragments is built up the tattered patchwork of the acrobat's personality at the moment of his fall.

In the third section the artist, now enlightened by the revelation of his past, recognizes the source of his own weakness. When he should step confidently along the wire his legs are stiff with pride and fear, crippled by the burden of the past which he carries with him. In despair he, the would-be saviour, stretches out his arms for help, and a child teaches him the way. Hand in hand they walk towards a lighted city, beautiful with starlight and the aimless enjoyments of art. Brought home to the promised land familiar to him in dreams, he recognizes it as the madhouse—the secret city glimpsed by children, known only to those adults whom frenzy or drugs have liberated from the prison of the conventional world.

Nezval himself subsequently commented upon the genesis of this poem:

It was at a climax of emotional repression and desire for simplicity, of captivation by the spell of defenceless innocence—and under the unbearable pressure of the imagination's dark powers that one late evening by a spontaneous process *The Acrobat* was born—that phantom which plunges to the ground before my eyes like the fall of pride—he that will dictate amid the wreckage of a festival my own autobiography. The accident which led my steps to the city of madmen at a moment when all its windows were stained with the blood of the setting sun, this accident, and the confusion which it aroused in my imagination inspired a finale without which I cannot conceive either my subsequent life or poetry. Poetry, real poetry, is not, I now believe, anything else but a systematization of confusion.[1]

Nezval was particularly interested in exploring his own methods of composition, but to the reader of this poem nothing is more revealing than his choice of theme—that of art and the artist. As the poets of antiquity claimed to be initiated to their calling by the revelation of Dionysus with his grotesque following of nymphs and satyrs, so in Nezval's poem the modern artist is dedicated to his task by the revelation of his own secret life, the surrealist world operating by its own laws below the level of his conscious self.

Nezval's poem first appeared in a recently founded periodical *Fronta*, a journal with international aspirations and devoted primarily to functional art and constructivism. The editorial board included two young writers of whom much was to be heard in succeeding years, František Halas, a poet, and Bedřich Václavek, a literary critic. The work of both was strongly influenced by the poetists, and like the latter they were anti-traditionalist as a matter of course. On the other hand their work shows a reaction against the increasing individualism and anarchy of some poetist writing. 'We are tired of the individualist spirit whose culminating achievement is to throw overboard every doctrine and discipline: instead of rules it knows only mood . . .' The advent of this journal may be taken as a symptom of a shift in the tastes of the avantgardists, a move back from the pursuit of perfect freedom in art to the search for order. The swing tended to split still further the ranks of the poetists, and besides the trend back towards a more traditional view of art may be seen a tendency in the opposite direction, a desire to out-do even 'orthodox' poetism by the exploitation of surrealist fantasy, based on a growing awareness of Freudian literary techniques.

[1] Introduction to the second edition of *Most* (1927).

In 1927 Halas published his first book of verse entitled *Sepie (The Squid)*. He had in fact been contributing poems to the journals for some time, and had shown a development not unlike that of Seifert—through Proletarian to poetist verse. In this early work Halas had stressed his adherence to social causes and material betterment, treating with contempt the theme of art and its dreams. When the motif of social revolution had faded into the background of his poetry, he retained his distrust for art and its conflict with the 'real' world of man. In the title poem of his book, the squid, which escapes capture by hiding itself within the ink it expels, is like the poet seeking a way out from reality by the dreams and poetry he produces: but for him there is no escape. His dreams have foundered on the rock of the real world:

> At dawn a lighthouse keeper
> I gather up my swallows
> The dreams that stunned on impact
> will fly no more[1]

A motif which occurs repeatedly in Halas' poetry is the sense of loss—expressed often as the fading of visions, or in mystical, biblical terms:

> The truths
> as old as the wine Noah drew
> are all drunk dry
> and where to find the new[2]

The realist school of Wolker, writing in the immediate post-war era, had stressed the hope of a better future: accepting, indeed assisting at the burial of the old world, they fed on their blueprints of the new. Halas writes as one who is resigned to the loss of both old and new:

---

[1] Zrána strážce majáku
sbírám své vlaštovky
Sny narazily o hlavu
už nevzletí

[2] Pravdy ty
staré jak víno které stáčel Noe
jsou dopity
kde najít nové

dreams of the promised society have faded in the cold light of disillusion. His journey is a return from dreams to reality, from illusion to the wreckage of life as it is, a world in which men live as they can:

> We opened our mouths to the full
> like the silenced barrels of guns
> where birds have nested and a few poor flowers . . .[1]

Death and chaos were to be Halas' favourite themes: in this book they are expressed particularly with reference to the recent World War. In his youthful poems he had written as if the only reality were revolution. With the passing of the revolutionary phase the truest reality to him apparently became death, to which all things give way. As in the past he had felt art to be peripheral to the real world of social turmoil, so, in his present phase, he felt it inadequate to express the grander and more terrifying theme of death. Halas is the reverse of Nezval in his attitude to art: there are no poet-liberators in Halas' verse, and his attitude to his own poetry is laconic, distrustful, and ironical:

> Tormented by elusive words
> distrust uneasy grows
> men say it is the poets' fate
> who knows who knows[2]

The first edition of *Sepie* contained a number of poems of quite different style, inconsequential word games, childish fantasies, and poems, like '*Meteory*' ('Meteors'), where a theme provided merely a base for verbal pyrotechnics. Such verse was purest poetism, and contemporary critics lost no time in pointing out the debt of Halas to Nezval and Seifert, even to details of theme and treatment. It is notable that in later editions, Halas made drastic revisions in the text of *Sepie*,

---

[1] Otevřeli jsme ústa dokořán
podobná zmlklým hlavním děl
kde uhnízdili se ptáci a několik ubohých kvítků . . .

[2] Pak mám podezíravé oči
trápím se nepostihlými slovy
prý je to osud básniků
kdo ví kdo ví

the main effect of which was to drop the more obvious poetist pieces and to leave the book much starker in theme, hence closer in spirit to his subsequent work.

In the same year as *Sepie* there appeared a book of verse which caused a mild sensation. It was *Panichida* (*The Vigil*), the debut of a young writer called Vilém Závada. If the verse of the poetists was still to some extent a continuation of Proletarian art, with Závada there is a clear break: highly intellectual and consciously literary, he is something of a poet's poet, a connoisseur of horror and corruption, draining the cup of guilt, sin, and despair. Závada's personal poetry emphasizes the isolation of man (in exact reverse of Wolker's feeling for the solidarity of common humanity): cut off from his fellow men he walks the earth as a stranger, always searching for a haven where he will at last feel at home. Religion was clearly a fundamental impulse to Závada: the eternal abyss around him appeared as a product of a tortured conscience. Cut off by his nature from the love of God, the poet peers into the realm of hell, and writes the lyrics of wild hallucinations, hysteria, and vertigo. There are some graceful and charming verses in his book, but they are peripheral to the essential character of the work, as is well suggested by some of the titles—'In the Beginning', 'Fevers', 'Lost Paradise', 'The Earthquake', 'The Credo', 'Old Europe', 'Farewell Farewell'.

Nezval in his poems enjoyed exploring the horrors of childhood fantasy, and Halas the motif of death; but in this field none of the young writers could approach the refined brutality of Závada's style and his elegant dalliance with satanic horror, rendering by comparison the extravagances of the poetists as mild and disconcertingly harmless.

In some literary circles Závada's book was welcomed as marking the beginning of the end for the poetists. The joyful peals which had heralded their advent only a few years before were now, to the sensitive ears of the critics, fading into a death-knell, bringing comfort to all who had condemned the poetists' extravagance and frivolity. Nevertheless it was at this time, when the wind had apparently been taken out of the poetists' sails, that their contribution to the development of modern Czech poetry began to receive wide recognition even in conservative quarters. Critics praised them for their liberation of poetry from ideological bonds, for their experiments with form and technique, and their imaginative use of the subconscious world. In retrospect, the poetist phase was seen as a period of transition during which traditional Czech rococo had briefly reappeared in modern dress. On the other hand, the era heralded by Halas and Závada with its feeling of the labyrinth of the world, the prison of this temporary life in which man is an exile from eternity, the rejection of this world and the yearning for the liberating hand of death—all this appeared as a return to the spirit of Czech baroque.

In this way post-war Czech poetry fell neatly into a convenient sequence of phases; but, like many theoretical models constructed by literary historians, this tells less than the truth. A phase was indeed passing, but poetism as a style was far from dead. Its founders had stressed from the outset that they were not founding a school but setting a style which could be followed or adapted by writers of very different stamp. In the light of fresh literary developments, Teige and Nezval now attempted to define their position in papers published in the new *Devětsil* journal, *ReD*. Teige wrote:

> Poetism was proclaimed not to take the place of some other artistic, literary or musical -ism: we wanted merely to formulate a view and define a trend.... Poetism was a way out of an embarrassing aesthetic and philosophical confusion and offering a fresh aesthetic and philosophical viewpoint....If it has in addition become a school and a system of poetics, it was neither the will nor the fault of its founders. Poetism as a school is meeting the fate of all schools: it has found its artists and imitators, it has lived through several superficial changes of fashion. . . . This poetism is nothing but a corrupt off-shoot of poetism as an attitude and an aesthetic prognosis.

Teige recalled the background to his first manifesto—his conviction of the sterility of Proletarian art, especially as laid down by Lunačarsky in Russia, contrasting with such ideological pamphleteering the imaginative work of a real revolutionary like Nezval. Where others were mere rhetoricians and apostles of revolution, he was above all a poet. Teige traced the pedigree of modernist poetry back to the romanticism of Baudelaire, and gave his analysis of its essential characteristics. In the first place there was an increasing tendency towards 'pure' poetry, that is, poetry freed from the incubus of alien elements such as moral guidance, ideology, history, etc. The purification of its content was accompanied by a liberation of form. The main source of its inspiration ceased to be the world of ideas and reason: intuition, fantasy, and the subconscious world of the human mind took their place as the raw material of art. At the same time an appreciation was developing of the interdependence of the senses and their artistic expression, so that music, painting, and literature were drawing closer together, and becoming more capable of combination in new art-forms.

From this analysis of Teige one might conclude that the trend would culminate in an art of pure form, devoid of logical aim or content and appealing to all the senses, combining sound, colour, harmony of form and rhythm with the fantasy of the human imagination.

Continuing in the line marked out by Mallarmé and Apollinaire we have passed through the new phase of pictorial poetry and thence to a new form of film art, to pure lyric cinography . . . to the fusion of poetry liberated from literature, and the picture liberated by cubism from imagery, to the identification of the poet and the painter. With this identification the history of painting concludes—painting in the sense and function attributed to it in the Middle Ages, painting as the profession of imagery, is condemning itself to death.

In the light of his own wide interests Teige saw literature only within the general context of art. Convinced that poetry in the traditional sense was as out of touch with the technical world of the twentieth century as was medieval painting, he saw the poetry of the future as a form of art different in kind from traditional literature, even as the pictures of Picasso differed in kind from those of Giotto. Art in the traditional sense was dead, since the conditions which had called it into being had passed. Representational painting and epic versifying had lost their function in the days of the camera and the gramophone: traditional painting and literature now belonged to the museum, together with other relics of the dead past. The only future for poetry was as a harmonizer of the arts, an expression of all five senses, a reconciler of 'higher' and 'lower' art, and it was thus that poetism had been conceived. In the words of Nezval, poetism was a way of looking at the world so as to transform it into a poem.

In retrospect many of Teige's ideas seem curiously utopian. The poster poems and optical effects which seemed to him to herald a new art-form, turned out to be merely a passing fad: the cinema—that great hope of the poetists—with its natural capacity to harmonize movement, sound, and colour, was slow to progress beyond the stage of shallow sensationalism. Poetry, in fact, instead of disappearing as an independent branch of art, continued to be written for the small minority who still wanted it. Its themes were changing all the time, and the new phase represented by Halas and Závada marked a change of mood among the younger writers, a swing back to traditional themes of death and damnation.

A basic characteristic of poetist verse, especially visible in the work of Nezval, was an exaltation of life for its own sake, a neurotic obsession with vigour, youth, and energy. But a conscious feeling for life implies a heightened consciousness of death. The traditional Epicurean motto 'Eat, drink, and be merry . . .' necessarily entails the conclusion ' . . . for tomorrow we die.' It is the death theme which now becomes a focus of their extravagant enthusiasm. When Nezval in 1930 published a collection of his recent work, he appropriately entitled it *Poems of the Night*.

The most significant inclusion was a long lyric-epic poem on the unpromising theme of the American inventor Edison. It was at first conventionally interpreted by the critics as a hymn to the technical miracles of the twentieth century, a belated expression of constructivist art. But actually the poem has little to say about the real Edison, and the only prolonged biographical excursus is the weakest section of the poem. The theme, once again, is that of the poet-liberator, but this time he appears no longer as a circus trickster but as a scientist with power to change the face of the earth. By his invention of the incandescent globe the new Prometheus is able to transform darkness to light, surpassing the wonders of fairy tales and dreams.

The contrast between light and darkness is a *leitmotif* of the poem, and the physical transformation is symbolic of the struggle between life and death, hope and despair. In the poem Nezval, wandering through Prague by night, encounters a would-be suicide who leads him in thought to the inventor. Edison appears in the poem as a Hamlet-like person wavering between the intoxication of creative genius and paroxisms of despair. A split personality, he embraces life at one moment and flees from it the next: the tension is emphasized by the constant repetition of the light-darkness transformation, the effect being driven home by a stream of images:

> And ever with renewed vitality
> you live and work by mania possessed
> You saw one day in Pennsylvania
> by Baker's side the arc-lamp and the dark
> and then you felt like me the poignant ache
> of one who writes his novel's final page
> like acrobat who crossed the tightrope wire
> like mother as she sees her new-born child
> like fisherman who draws a loaded net
> like lover when he moves from soft embrace

like soldiers marching from the battle home
like earth at vintage when its grapes are gone
like star that fades amid the glowing dawn
like man whose shadow suddenly is lost
like God that made the rose the night the bane
like God that yearned to form undreamed-of words
like God that must for ever mould afresh
new vessels forming with creative hand
descending from the mists upon the land[1]

There is no logical development of theme, only a sequence of moods, as
the imagination, led on by sound, flies from image to image until the
touch of a familiar chord closes the circle of association:

One evening in October of that year
sunk deep in sombre thought you paced along
within the Menlo Park laboratory
your little gifts and letters all around
and as your fingers absently revolved
the little mill in dreaming reverie
from threads of carbon suddenly they shaped
the bird whose eyes watch with us through the night
the scourge that drives away the monstrous shades
the glowing vision of the dreaming walks
the angel set above the gable end

---

[1] Vždycky znovu žít a míti manii
jedenkrát jste uzřel v Pensylvanii
noc a obloukovou lampu u Bakera
pocítil jste smutek tak jako já včera
nad poslední stránkou svého románu
jako akrobat jenž přešel po lanu
jako matka která porodila dítě
jako rybář který vytáh plné sítě
jako milenec po sladké rozkoši
jako z bitev kráčející zbrojnoši
jako země v poslední den vinobraní
jako hvězda která hasne za svítání
jako člověk náhle ztrativší svůj stín
jako Bůh jenž stvořil růži noc a blín
jako Bůh jenž toužil stvořit nová slova
jako Bůh jenž musí tvořit vždycky znova
hněta z svého dechu nové kalichy
snášeje se s vodou oblak na líchy

the roses circling restaurants cafés
the fountains sparkling down dark boulevards
the rosary above the river bridge
the halo of the ladies of the night
the garlands draped above the funnelled ships
the tears that stream from high aloft to ground
above the muffling city catafalque
above the mummified cathedral shapes
above the flitting souls in café smoke
above the eternal ice of mirrored wine
above the catafalque of city mists
above my spirit's torn discordant strings
on which I play and beg for lights
for dreams for love—and weeping change the masks
with passion of a minstrel old a prince
the ruler of Balmoral's frenzied town
through whose fair gate in dreams I ever move
between the sombre ranks of captive serfs
of murdered princes raging dancing bands
of madness driving on beribboned wheels
of bells that toll sadistic passions' knell
of hovering chimeras through the dark
a drinker-in of charm and bloody foam
a drinker-in of grinding viciousness
of life and death's regret and loneliness[1]

[1] Večer na začátku října tentýž rok
sklíčen odměřoval jste svůj vážný krok
po laboratoři v slavném Menloparku
uprostřed své korespondence a dárků
toče prsty mlýnek v snění ze zvyku
uhnětl jste maně z vláken uhlíku
ptáka našich nocí s kterým dlouho bdíme
metlu příšer stínů jíž je zaháníme
žhavé poletuchy snivých promenád
anděla nad štíty nároží a vrat
růže restaurantů kaváren a barů
vodotrysky noci ve tmách na bulváru
růžence nad mosty velkoměstských řek
aureolu pouličních nevěstek
věnce nad komíny velkých parolodí
slzy které kanou s výšin nad poschodí
nad katafalk města které tlumí je
nad budovy chrámů staré mumie
nad kavárny v nichž jsou plytké duše v dýmu

Nezval has been described as the poet of intoxication, the 'possessed' artist who surrendered absolutely to his inner demon, a demon which could be aroused by a mere association of sound or image. His peculiar gifts marked him out as the most elemental, unrestrained and at times naive of all modern Czech poets. The logic of the world and its burden of moral problems which loom large in the work of Hora and Závada can hardly be found in Nezval. Consequently his work lacks some of their humanity, but is freer and less encumbered. When Teige wrote of modern poetry reaching a climax in pure art disassociated with logic or morals, it was Nezval whom he had in mind, but the new, mature Nezval who could combine the fantasy of self-hypnosis with a mastery of poetic technique which in fact was the product of discipline in composition.

The book *Poems of the Night* included an impressionist poem, '*Neznámá ze Seiny*' ('The Unknown Girl taken from the Seine'). It was typical of Nezval in his new mood that he should select as a theme the vision of a drowned girl floating down the river of Paris, the poetists' dreamland which Nezval had never seen. The opening of the poem is a charming picture of the Seine at evening:

> Bright like a gleaming topaz
> glitters the water The maidens
> step to the waist in the river
> Friends from the homes by the Seine

> nad zrcátka vín nad jejich věčnou zimu
> nad katafalk města mdlobných výparů
> nad mou duši rozladěnou kytaru
> na níž jako žebrák světel snů a lásky
> vyhrávám a pláči proměňuje masky
> s vášní truvéra já princ a bludný král
> města orgií jež sluje Balmorál
> jehož slavnou branou vcházím vždycky ve snu
> černým kordónem svých poddaných a vězňů
> knížat vražd a hysterických karmaňol
> drožek šílenství a opentlených kol
> sadistických vášní při nichž znějí zvony
> chimér vzlétajících z ložnic nad balkóny
> piják krutých hazardních a krásných žen
> piják rozkoše a zkrvavělých pěn
> piják všeho krutého co štve a drtí
> piják hrůz a smutku z života i smrti

3. 'The poet-clown', an illustration by F. Tichý to the book, V. Nezval: *Kůň a tanečníce* (*The Horse and the Dancer*, a collection of Nezval's poems, edited by F. Tichý).

4. Cover, designed by Karel Teige, of Seifert's collection, *On Waves of Radio*, 1925.

join in the song of the girls
singing like sirens and thinking
still as they sing of the fishermen
wrapped in the blue of the haze
folded in afternoon mist[1]

The Parisian girls who walk beside the river are symbolic of radiant
youth, but the water is a mirror which transforms youthful charm into
the corruption of death:

Hands as they wash feel the tender
touch of the lily's caress
Clear their reflection that mirrors
as in a glass where their fleeting
years pass away with the fishes
as in a glass where the maidens
turn into women grown haggard[2]

The beguiling song of the sirens changes into a death-knell as a corpse
comes gently floating down the stream:

There in the marble-like darkness
as in a shell lies a body
a little dead girl in a boat
little dead drowned naked woman
flying spray sullies her pallor
foam like the delicate corner
edging the train of a garment
frozen the smile on her features
set like the smile on a death-mask
smile that has paid off for ever

---

[1] Voda třpytí se jak nejvzácnější topas
pradlenky se do ní noří téměř po pas
jejich přítelkyně z domků od Seiny
prozpěvují s nimi jako sirény
zpívají a myslí při tom na rybáře
zahalené v modré odpolední páře

[2] leknín líbá jejich ruce při prádle
odrážejí se v něm jako v zrcadle
v kterém plynou jejich léta s rybkami
v kterém stávají se dívky babkami

F

claims due to death as to love
coaxing it forth like a swan-song
offering her smile as the wounded
pour out their blood to the ground[1]

Taken from life at the moment of physical maturity, the dead girl is a
human sacrifice: upon the symbol of her virginity, the floating white
pinafore, the power of the sun beats relentlessly. Her appearance
leads the poet inexorably towards his main theme, the fascination of
all-powerful death:

> Death saw you turn from that sorrow
> grief that embroiled you in currents
> sweeping you down the morass
> driving you on like a fever
> on like a tempest like hunger
> death the superb like tremendous
> waterfall set in the mountains
> dazzling the eye like a serpent
> rotting away like the marshland
> grim like a towering castle
> death like a talisman haunting
> temples submerged by the waters
> seal that I kiss—seal that I break
> leaving your purple-decked cities
> leaving your mirrors and stars[2]

---

[1] V mramorové noci jako v skořápce
leží malá mrtvá dívka v kocábce
leží malá nahá utonulá žena
jejíž bledost třísní zenitová pěna
jako řídký cípek vlečky oděvu
jejíž malá ústa ztuhla v úsměvu
trvalém jak úsměv na posmrtné masce
v úsměvu jenž platil smrti jako lásce
který loudila jak labut' loudí zpěv
jako dává poraněný zemi krev

[2] Odvrátila jsi se v smrti od žalu
který zavedl tě k proudům močálu
jako choroba jak vichřice jak hlad
Smrti nádherná jak horský vodopád
oslňující svou korunou jak had

In the thought and imagery of the new Nezval were to be seen not only the current pre-occupations of the poetists but also his own reading of Edgar Allan Poe, whose 'Raven' he had recently translated. In the collection *Poems of the Night* Nezval included two other poems of similar mood. One of these was entitled simply *'Noci'* ('To the Night') in which the poet explored the depths of horror and nostalgia proper to the theme of darkness. The other poem was *'Silvestrovská noc'* ('The Night of New Year's Eve'). Whereas *'Noci'* was, according to Nezval, written as an automatic text under the influence of his own impressions on a walk through old Prague, *'Silvestrovská noc'* was a carefully planned poem, perhaps under the influence of Poe's essay 'The Philosophy of Composition'. The poem expresses the feelings of horror inspired by the sight of a girl's hand lying on the poet's desk as he works through the night, a hand which brings a summons of death. 'The phantom of a paper-weight of a girl's hand, which comes to terrify a man who has, as he thinks, found his own home—this is the materialization of one of those obsessive feelings that clearly spring from my old fears of night which I shall never lose . . . '[1] Nowhere did Nezval approach more closely to the spirit of Poe than in *Poems of the Night* with all its atmosphere of spectres and wild hallucinations, collapsing ruins and open graves, and the artist working under the spell of supernatural horror.

But sepulchral gloom was but one element in the irrepressible Nezval's capacious repertoire. His new book of personal lyrics *Hra v kostky* (*Dice*) included poems written up to 1928, verses of poetist elegance and fantasy but with a graveyard atmosphere which imparted a not unpleasant touch of the macabre. A typical example of the new Nezval was the title poem in the section *'Album'*.

> In autumn time when swinging park-gates creak
> and steps are pressing on the muddy tracks
> of columns moving to the cemetery
> when amid the throng her weaving laid aside

> trouchnivá jak močál děsivá jak hrad
> smrti talismane potopených chrámů
> pečeti již líbám pečeti již lámu
> odvracím se od tvých purpurových měst
> odvracím se od tvých zrcadel a hvězd

[1] Introduction to *Most*.

a woman hurries old and bent—
an antique album smells with the wild thyme's scent
and a child is fingering its pages through

The pictures—sad with far-off women's lonely scent
in autumn time when walls are stained with damp
like the vanished perfume of the wedding dress
of the old hag hastening towards the grave[1]

The pages of the album link the child with the old woman stumbling
through the mud to visit the grave to which she already half belongs:

In the leaden misty autumn time the old
have left their graveyard candles moving home
beneath their shawls of grey they huddle cold
on crutches never realizing that
within the album's covers they have left
the freshness of their youth The bells resound
and praying for her grandchildren each goes
on muddy tracks across the soaking loam
and hurries on her stick towards her home
and creakingly the swinging park-gates close[2]

[1] V ten podzimní čas kdy skřípají v parcích vrata
a kroky na zemi pod šlépějemi bláta
v nichž táhnou průvody po cestě k hřbitovu
kdy shrbená stařenka s poutníky chvátá
když vysoukala osnovu
zavoní staré album jako máta
a dítě listuje v něm zas a poznovu

Obrázky s tesknou vůní dávných žen
v ten podzimní čas kdy stéká vlhko stěn
jak zašlý parfum ze svatebních šatů
té stařenky jež spěchá na hřbitůvek v chvatu

[2] V ten podzimní čas jak z mlh a olova
se berou stařenky od svíček z hřbitova
schouleny zimavě pod šedou loktuší
a jdouce o berli svou cestou netuší
že zanechaly v albu jako v lázni
svá svěží těla a když zvony zazní
s křižováním se modlí za vnoučata
a každá domů o berličce chvátá
po mokré zemi s šlépějemi bláta
a v parcích skřípavě se zavírají vrata

Nezval later described the book as a repository of chance memories, a mirror thoughtlessly raised to passing life, a book based on momentary impulses and the inspiration of changing or self-contradictory feelings, an atmosphere of dusty souvenirs, a graceful touch of the picture postcard and the sentimental refrain. In the spirit of the times Nezval had now turned his back on the principles of anarchy in form, and wrote according to the closely organized model of the classical rondel:

> Forgive my kissing you in spirit more
> than your magnificence permits
> A kiss—a dove released by Noah
> why pluck its feathers as it flits
>
> It fled—as when a nun a novice pure
> her convent cell for ever quits
> Forgive my kissing you in spirit more
> than your magnificence permits . . .[1]

In the same collection appears a poem which combines the familiar themes of nostalgic reminiscence, fading masks and peeling gilt, set in an autobiographical setting:

> When I am old and stoop above the plots
> within the glass-house fine-spun veils conceal
> and standing at the stove you hear the bells
> from clock-towers in the distant cities peal
>
> alone without one grandchild—you will slip
> past curtains to that secret room of mine
> where hang the wreaths with fading tones
> of benzoin chypre basalik and thyme
>
> where faded wreaths my loves bizarre proclaim
> and combs and silk and masks a still-life frame . . .[2]

---

[1] Odpust' mi že tě líbám v duchu více
než dovolí mi tvoje nádhera
Polibek—Noemova holubice
Nač strhovat ji v letu za péra

Už vyběhl jak malá řeholnice
opouštějící kobku kláštera
Odpust' mi že tě líbám v duchu více
než dovolí mi tvoje nádhera . . .

The collection *Hra v kostky* was among the most charming which Nezval ever produced. Its appeal lay in its great variation of theme and mood, its intelligibility for the general reader, and in the mastery of poetic technique which gave it the impress of maturity and polish. The old forms of verse were typical of the book's whole atmosphere of past associations, as though the intricate game of poetism had moved into a gracious Bohemian drawing room, where the passage of time was punctuated only by the ticking of old clocks and the elegant strains of the minuet. If this was the end of poetism, it was, at first sight, a strange and narrow world for revolutionaries to attain. Yet from the beginning the modernists had abhorred nothing in literature so much as the pretentiousness of heroism and tragedy, and in the soul-searching atmosphere of the late twenties a last defence for sanity lay in the gift of nonchalance and the cult of irony.

---

[2] Až budu stár sklánět se nad záhony
v skleníku skrytém v jemné závoje
ty budeš nad plotnou poslouchat v dálce zvony
jež odbíjejí v městech z orloje

bez vnoučat sama—vklouzneš za záclony
do mého tajemného pokoje
kde budou viset věnce s mdlými tóny
bazalek chypru máty benzoe

ty zvadlé věnce bizarních mých lásek
zátiší z hřebenů hedvábí a masek . . .

6

THE SEARCH

IN 1929 Konstantin Biebl, the former Proletarian writer, published a new book of verse entitled *Nový Ikaros* (*The New Icarus*), which received a publisher's prize. The award was made not only for the book's intrinsic quality but also because, in the view of the judges, it represented the outlook and experience of the generation whose adolescence had been spent in wartime. Its members were no longer young rebels, clamouring to be heard, but writers of consequence whose views were now received with respect, and who had already established an orthodoxy of their own. Their starting point was the Great War, once seen as an act of national vindication: in literature it had now become accepted as the symbol of ultimate futility. The writers had constructed a mythology of the past in which they appeared as a generation robbed of full development. Plunged into a fiery ordeal at the beginning of their youth, they had been children in the pre-war world; and were aliens in the post-war world. Like neurotics who seek to bury memories they dare not face, they succeeded only in awakening everywhere the memories of their past.

Biebl's long poem (it ran to sixty pages) was a rather formless epic, written in the surrealist style then becoming popular in France. Unlike a classic epic it had no plot or denouement, was strung on a thread not of action but of consciousness, and was intensely personal poetry. It was the fantasy life of Biebl himself, and, but for its length and lack of form, would rather be classed as a lyric poem. It began with fragments of childhood recollection: the symbol of lost security was the protecting wings of the guardian angel, so familiar to the Czech nursery tale. From the nursery's comforting lamp it was a step to the memory of tropical nights in Biebl's travels—forked lightning over the boundless ocean, and crabs crawling from below the earth over the slimy rocks.

The quick switch, and the contrast between the sanctuary of childhood and the menace of foreign, endless distances was typical of the poem's style. In his usual way Biebl filled his poem with waving palms, lighted ships, exotic birds, and sleeping coolies; all this colourful paraphernalia of tropical life was brought into contrast with the familiar scenes of home, disfigured by war. The thread of association which guided the thought was tenuous, the impression given was chaotic: Ceylon and its elephants; the ivory horn; the last trump; the war dead; death in many forms; the buried past:

> We walked into the catacombs
> along the line of yawning graves
> amid the coffins' icy draught
> she took my hand . . .
>
> through the midst of ancient Rome I walk
> caressed by horror and the void. . . .[1]

From this elegant picture of decay the reader is conducted back to the idiot's delight of war, whose symbol is the drummer of death:

> The drummer beats the drum for the assault
> into the darkness and the void
> where all the dead are staring forward forward
> into the darkness and the void
>
> The drummer beats the drum the drum
> into the darkness and the void. . . .[2]

Like ancient Icarus who longed to fly, the poet seeks to break the bondage of space and time which pull him down to earth. Like Nezval's

---

[1] Šli jsme do katakomb
dlouhou řadou zívajících hrobů
tam v studeném průvanu rakví
vzala mne za ruku . . .
procházím vnitřnostmi starého Říma
objala mne prázdnota a hrůza . . .

[2] Bubnuje bubeník bubnuje k útoku do tmy a prázdna
kam všichni mrtvi se dívají kupředu kupředu do tmy a prázdna
Bubnuje bubeník bubnuje do tmy a prázdna. . . .

poet-acrobat he summons all his reserves of wit and daring for the adventure, which means escape from a living death to the uninhibited life of the imagination. Poetry will be his wings.

The futility of life and the vanity of human effort are motifs worn rather threadbare by poets of the nineteenth century. The saving grace of Biebl's poem was his use of poetist romanticism to express the disillusion fashionable in the 1930s. The feeling of spiritual disintegration was expressed in a disintegration of language. The autobiography of a generation was an interesting and ambitious subject; perhaps too ambitious for Biebl and his chosen method. To be convincing, a rapid movement from impression to impression depends on a mastery of the techniques of mental association and of paradox. Studied chaos is a very different thing to formlessness and mere caprice: to be a master of anarchy one must first be a master of ordered style. Biebl's work was marred by a carelessness of composition which critics were quick to point out. His poem in fact foreshadows the surrealist verse of the thirties—at times the raw material of poetry rather than poetry itself. It was also perhaps rather self-consciously dramatic, so that the reader was left with the uncomfortable suspicion of a pose. Yet by its quality the poem impressed so demanding a critic as Šalda, and it has survived where so much verse of that period of the time has been forgotten.

The long poem, however, is alien to modern taste, and was hardly an ideal medium for Biebl's lyric gifts. When the prize-giving jury commended the work as the life-story of a generation, they were in one way labelling it as an historical curiosity, to be read by later generations not so much for itself as for an insight into the pessimism and frustration of the poet's contemporaries.

Another book of verse, this time by Hora, appeared in 1929, dealing with the same subject. It was *Deset let* (*Ten Years*), also a retrospective survey of the post-war decade. A series of poetic sketches led from the theme of war to the days of the great return, with all its hopes, and the growth of social revolution as a movement and an idea. The fresh aspirations of men, glimpsing the abundance of the world's resources, provide a theme on which Hora enlarges in a style reminiscent of the poetists. His imagination flits like an albatross above far-bound ships and spans the earth's expanse from the mirage-haunted deserts of the South to the gleam of the Northern Lights. The hopes of humanity centre upon Russia, and the father-figure of Lenin. But gradually the voice of revolution falls silent:

The ships stand motionless,
the sirens' voice has faded into mist,
the lighthouses are dimmed . . .[1]

The welcoming light of the collective spirit, to which men had flocked
to escape the loneliness of their sterile lives, now is fading. The steps
which were to have led to a promised land now lead towards a new
precipice; across the plains which hide the recent dead, new armies are
on the march. Hope lies only in the eyes of children, who look into the
future, and see their own image.

Ten Years cannot be called a personal lyric, for the personality of the
writer is not allowed to obtrude: Hora's narrative is an expression of
the social sympathies of the generation of the early twenties: in its
social note and realist style it recalled the work of Wolker. The disillusion with the peace, which prepared the atmosphere for the poetry
of nihilism, also provided conditions for a return to the themes of social
revolt. In the same year Hora published another book of verse, *Mít
křídla* (*To have Wings*), even closer to the Proletarian tradition, and
containing such poems as 'Sacco and Vanzetti', and 'Ivan and Lenin'.
Hora's resumption of the social theme was not an isolated instance;
it was, as will be seen, taken up by other writers, though it did
not produce another successful wave of socially committed literature,
and never attained real popularity. It is perhaps significant that
both Hora's books were first published in 1929 in editions of only
120 copies.

Biebl, Hora, Seifert, and Nezval all reacted to the prevailing social
and psychological climate, according to their styles, in accents of social
indignation and morbid fantasy. But it was the younger generation,
Závada and Halas, who explored to its depths the chamber of horrors
in which they found their true literary domain. Outstanding in
its genre was Halas' new book, *Kohout plaší smrt* (*The Cock alarms
Death*), a collection of verse in which morbid fantasy and social
realism are both well represented. In the current fashion he includes
several poems on war themes—'Europe', 'The Battlefield', and 'The
Dead Man':

---

[1] Utkvělý lodi,
hlas sirén se rozprchl v mlze
majáky dohasínájí . . .

Upon the mantle of his blood he lies
His face—that mask—torn off by fear
Magic has opened his lifeless eyes . . .[1]

Like Závada, Halas draws near to the spirit of Catholic baroque art.
In the world of introspection death appears as larger than life; the
reality is death, and life is its pallid reflection. But unlike the Catholic
writers, Halas has no faith, or hope of grace, to save him. The only true
harmony is that of the human imagination; it is reality that lies upon it
as the disturbing element:

> The world grown so familiar
> lies on your dream
> The grub within the rose[2]

Halas notes his progressive dehumanization: the self has become the
shadow; the face a stream of masks; only in death does the true face
emerge. Halas has adopted death as his own domain and the graveyard
has become the centre of his poetic scenery:

Laugh at the shadow when still behind your back it crouches with terror
    senseless
Quickly death blows out the face's light
A new star kindling

Hark to the gentle crack its steps clear sounding
That crack we heard at combing of women's flowing hair
At each love's dying

In dirt and gravel lies our life
Then shed no tears for loss of serpent's crown
The earth feels us no more

---

[1] Translated by E. Osers and J. K. Montgomery:

> Leží na mantile krve své
> škrabošku tváře strhl strach
> tajným klíčem otevřeny oči vyhaslé . . .

[2] Svět tak známý až je cizí
> leží na tvém snu
> Plž skrytý v růži

A thousand times we drank of happiness and swallowed only death
Betrothed to graves a voice is calling
Above the vigil of the cocks at crowing
Amid the hollowness of night the horn of plenty lies unseen
Death empties it and the corpse with a star in its mouth
Cries out for the boon of sleep
Through the graveyard poisons seep by heaven rejected
Christ to green corroded lies in death
By crouching shadows' images anew betrayed[1]

It would be hard to say what external causes contributed most to the note of pessimism which pervades much of European imaginative literature of the early thirties. The gathering economic storm which culminated in the great depression has commonly been blamed. Actually the financial crisis took some time to reach Czechoslovakia, and there the blackest literary mood predated its effect by several years. But the literary climate of gloom and near-panic was infectious in Europe; and a close examination of book sales might confirm the writers' early apprehensions. In the immediate aftermath of war, literary journals had multiplied, and book sales had soared; that stage had long passed, and the market for literature was shrinking. Journals foundered; books

---

[1] Vysmát se stínu když za zády se krčí strachy bez sebe
smrt rychle zhasí tvář
a novou hvězdu rozžehne

Naslouchejte něžnému praskotu jejích čistých kroků
ten praskot slýchávali jsme při česání dlouhých vlasů žen
za umírání lásek

V kamení hlíně zasuto je žití naše
pro ztrátu hadí koruny své hlavy neplačte
ta země nás už necítí

Tisíckrát polykajíce štěstí polkli jsme jen smrt
nápadníci hrobů hlas volá
přes bdělost kohoutů za kuropění

V dutině noci nepovšimnut leží roh hojnosti
smrt jej vysypává a umrlec v ústech hvězdu
milosti spánku se dovolává

Hřbitov je nassát jedy nebesa nikdy je nepřijmou
Kristus rozežraný měděnkou dotrpěl
přízraky shrbených stínů znovu prodávají jej

were published in tiny editions and remained unsold. The young artists, who had once flexed their muscles as the leaders of men and the heralds of a new age, now found their services redundant. The time of hope was over; something had gone terribly wrong with the world. The writers, instead of looking into a bright future, now began to look backwards towards their starting-point.

A decade after the armistice had been signed, the Great War had become a central topic in literature. Remarque's book, *All Quiet on the Western Front*, translated into many languages, was but one of the books which recalled the war theme with the accent on horror and futility. Thoughts of death are, after all, not uncommon in imaginative literature at all times, and do not necessarily spring from social causes, but the pessimism of this time extended over a wider area than that occupied by the artists. Spengler's *Decline of the West* was becoming popular reading even among people with no interest in the philosophy of history. The popularity of books of this nature suggests that they satisfied a contemporary taste for vistas of ruin, and a feeling that Europe had entered the twilight of its existence. Among the Czech writers the avantgardists were as unrestrained as ever in their gloom, and had already begun with enthusiasm to embrace the themes of nihilism. But it is interesting to note how much their mood was shared by the older generation of writers with whom the avantgardists had generally been at odds. The later work of poets like V. Dyk is touched with a pessimism less spectacular, but in some ways more chilling, than that of their younger contemporaries. The survivors of nineteenth-century Decadence returned to the literary scene, and J. Karásek, still waving his satanic and sadistic banners, published in 1930 a new book of sick verse, *Písně tulákovy o životě a smrti* (*A Vagabond's Songs of Life and Death*).

The veteran poet J. S. Machar, after serving the state in a high capacity for years, in 1931 returned to the literary scene with a prose poem entitled *Peníze* (*Money*) in which he pictured contemporary society as utterly corrupted by greed and the struggle for power. In the pages of right-wing—as of left-wing—writers, contemporary Czechoslovakia began to appear as a Sodom ripe for destruction: Catholic writers like Durych used their talents to flay the Establishment for its lack of principles, its vacillating pragmatism, and its cultural impotence.

Pragmatism as a philosophy had spread from America to Europe, and a whole school of Czech prose writers and intellectuals became identified with it. They were commonly regarded as echoing an official line in literature, and such favour as they gained in high circles earned them the reputation of being defenders of the *status quo*. In public life the pragmatists won great credit for their businesslike methods, their commonsense, and their talent for compromise; and they undoubtedly enhanced the international reputation of their country. But when reflected in literature their qualities seemed less inspiring, and the taint of official approval which hung about their work was enough to condemn it in the eyes of the rebels. The latter could no longer be shrugged off as parlour revolutionaries. They included Marxists, and former Marxists, who once had believed that a new world could be created out of the ashes of the old by means of faith working with science. But they also included men whose social ideals were subordinate to their religious faith. The quality which joined this heterogeneous collection of artists and thinkers was their search for a faith. The paroxysms of guilt and remorse of the Catholic mystics in literature were matched by the doubts and disillusion of the political revolutionaries whose social hopes had been eroded by time.

Ever since the Russian revolution, news from Moscow had been avidly scanned by those who saw in the Communist experiment the hope of mankind. Hopes faded, as the golden age did not appear; and the early era of artistic experimentation in Russia was succeeded by one of increasing dogmatism. In 1930, when the economic depression in Western Europe was providing conditions suitable for the Popular Front in politics, many Western writers were eager to join forces with their Russian counterparts and produce work with a socially-committed standpoint. How far they were out of touch with Russian conditions was shown when they met at Kharkov to found the so-called World Congress of Proletarian Writers. There the Rappists (as they soon became known) attempted to put their organization on an international basis by founding affiliations abroad. In peremptory fashion the Russian convenors demanded a definite committment to Marxism, and a determination on the part of all writers to make their work part of their revolutionary practice. As a final goal they demanded the handing over of all literary production to the working class.

The results of the Rappists' campaign in Western Europe were predictably minimal. A Rappist branch was organized in Prague, but no writers of consequence joined it. The rift between the avantgardists and the Marxist literary pundits had been steadily widening, and in 1929 an open quarrel had led to the expulsion of several writers from the Communist Party. They included three poets: Neumann, Hora, and Seifert.

Their work was officially condemned by the Communists, and members were instructed not to read them. The unity of the 'progressive' artists was shattered, together with their hopes. Disillusion was complete, and the believers in social revolution ended in greater pessimism than their pragmatic counterparts. From celebrating the sweets of life in poetist intoxication they turned to the worship of death. Their symbols, the harlequin and the circus ring, now became the sexton and the charnel house. As they fell out of love with life, so their exaltation of man's creativity turned into a morbid exploration of his darkest and most sinister aspects, utilizing a primitive Freudism as a guide to their study of the psyche.

The master of graveyard lyrics was Halas, whose new book of verse, *Tvář* (*The Face*), appeared in 1931. Stylistically his poems are among the more difficult in Czech; his extreme economy of phrase and over-worked syntax make him hard to comprehend, even more to translate. This close compression does not make for instant appeal: he has been described as a master of anacoluthon, and the intellectual effort required to understand his poetry is such that one marvels at his success with the public. But in *The Face* there was less cultivation of ugliness, in sound and rhyme, than in his earlier work: the song of the cemetery is not without its own charm:

> You'll smell the roses down below
> as you live your death-life through
> and cast into the dark the love
> shielding you

> And I the ivy round your grave
> the quiet song's embrace
> a parchment you have written things
> time will not efface

> We shall sleep together once again
> and the wind through the reeds will moan aloud
> we shall hear the lapping of Lethe's stream
> the women singing as they soak the shroud[1]

---

[1] Zezdola k růžím přivoníš
až budeš smrt svou žít
a do tmy lásku odhodíš
svůj štít

Love had now become a more important theme in Halas' art; inevitably
it is linked with the theme of decay: spring's first carefree rapture is the
icy warning of the winter which will extinguish its blossoms for ever:

> Silent and still your body is
> my trembling eyelids all its weeping know
> How silent and how still your body is[1]

The poem happily combines the themes of sex and death: Halas'
graveyard lyrics commonly wear the seal of sensuality. As in the case of
the poetists, his pre-occupation with the tomb was that of the hedonist
who regrets the transience of life's consolations, and his resignation had
the tone of a voluptuous surrender. Halas' poetry, compact in expression and loaded in meaning, is full of introspection and moral
conflict: it reveals how far the poetist wave had rolled from the playful
rococo of its early days. It seems at times as though he had fallen in love
with his own inner struggle, and that this was his new form of romanticism. The issues at stake were not always clear: critics have interpreted them as a conflict between the self-will of the artist and the imposed ethic of the group, the tension between Halas the poet and Halas
the Marxist. The overall impression which he gives is one of alienation
—in ideology as well as in art; the world of his ideas, beliefs, and hopes
is fading away, and the poet feels himself as part of it. In his private
world the paths are broken: steps can move neither backwards, to the
remembered world of childhood, nor forwards, in painful search for a
new way. In his love poems Halas shows a curious preoccupation with
the ceremony or ritual of love; his grave poems have at times the overtones of a prayer. Závada had brought the work of the avantgardists

---

U paty hrobu budu břečt'anem
tichou písní co tě obklíčí
popsaný tebou pergamen
který čas nezničí

Zas budem spolu spát
na syrinx trav nám vichry zahrají
šplounání Lethe budem naslouchat
a písni pradlen když rubáš máchají

[1] Přetiché je tělo tvé
jeho pláč zachvívá mými víčky
jak tiché je tělo tvé

nearer to that of the Catholic poets, but it was Halas who bridged the gulf, and helped to unite two rich traditions in modern Czech literature.

In 1931 perhaps the greatest, and certainly the most original, writer of Catholic mysticism was Jakub Deml. Born in 1878, and ordained as a priest, he had left the service of the church in 1909, and spent most of his life feuding with its living officers. He had a gift for invective, and a positive talent for making enemies. For years he lived in dire poverty on the charity of his admirers, whose numbers were perpetually diminished by his shafts of bitter scorn. He carried free verse so far that it is difficult at times to know whether he was intending to write verse or lyrical prose. Deml's contempt for readers and critics has met a not unexpected reward in almost total neglect, and even today his work is known to few readers. His poetry is filled with visions of hell and evil, which he pictured as a great beast pouncing upon, and from within mankind. As a Christian he accepts the call to sacrifice and death; Calvary becomes a promised land, and the crown of thorns the object of his passionate embrace. A feature of Deml's imaginary world is the idea of home—not the homely soil of his native Moravia but the mystical focus of his attachments: 'Never, never am I downcast. Look, the wealth that lies within my house! Within its rooms are my kinsmen, unto the fourth generation backwards and forwards. Below, within the cellars, my friends are at feast. *The wine is mine* . . . .'

Like the Expressionists, Deml wrote often from the standpoint of a child. In his *Castle of Death* the mother, identified as the nation, slays her child—that is, art; and without it there can be no future generations: life becomes nothing but an organism composed of chemical fertilizers and political faiths. The poet's eye is the eye of the child, uncorrupted by imposed systems: without wonder there can be no poetry. In the style of the nineteenth-century Romanticists Deml identifies himself with all sentient things. His long and painful pilgrimage is sustained by his feeling for an all-embracing unity. His imagery is drawn from the immense bounty of nature:

It was night. I opened the window. The storm had long passed; fine rain was falling, and the air was still. The threads of rain were sparkling in delicate, endless rhythm through the May night between heaven and earth before my window . . . as though taut in a frame, and trembling in unseen hands: or as if someone had set our house at the proper distance from a great musical instrument of nature, rustling in intimate melody. . . .

G

Deml wrote a good deal of his work in later life in the decades between the wars. Yet in one sense his work belongs to an earlier era. It is connected with later writing chiefly by the influence he had on younger writers, especially on Nezval, who always declared his allegiance to the master. In Nezval's opinion Deml, by his exploration of the sub-conscious world in poetry, was the true forerunner, in Czech literature, of the surrealists. Close to him in spirit are the poets of damnation, Závada and Halas; but his true heir, as the spokesman of Catholic mysticism, was a young writer who began to publish only in 1930 and gained rapid favour with his books *Pokušení smrti* (*The Temptation of Death*) and *Návrat* (*The Return*). It was Jan Zahradníček, a poet who lacked the depth and originality of Deml, but far outshone him in popularity, won to a large extent by his appealing lyrical style. The raw material of his poetry is the familiar cult of darkness and death, the redeeming stigmata of the crucifixion, the brooding mystery of the supernatural, and the ecstatic vision of lost spiritual horizons. With the advent of Zahradníček it seemed indeed that the spirit of Symbolism and Decadence had returned to the throne of Czech literature, and the glories of the 1890s would live again.

Nezval's contribution to the poetic chamber of horrors was a sequel to his earlier poem '*Edison*'. It was the long poem '*Signál času*' ('Time Signal'), on the death of the inventor: the man whose miracles had transformed darkness into light now is himself extinguished for ever. The central theme is death; the poem is punctuated by the time signal which marks the passing of human life. The setting was the half-conscious mind of the poet; in his characteristic manner Nezval drew the material for his poetry from his own dreams and fantasies. 'Time Signal' was included by him as the introductory poem to a new collection of verse with the strange title of *Skleněný havelok* (*The Glass Cape*). The idea is drawn from a novel of the surrealist poet André Breton: behind his covering of glass the inner part of men is exposed as a constant stream of desires, hopes, fantasies, and feelings which lie beneath the surface of his own consciousness, like the mass of the iceberg which floats beneath the water. Although the Prague Surrealist Group was not formed until 1934, after Nezval's return from Paris, his work had shown much in common with that of the surrealists from early days. The borderland of the mind had for long been the native climate of Nezval's poetry; but whereas in his earlier work the dreams had been often of the fairy tale variety, from now on they became more like nightmares, obsessed with gloom, madness, and terror.

The opening poem of his new collection, *Pět prstů* (*Five Fingers*), is 'The History of Six Empty Houses'. The first house is that of the womb; the setting is a church; his mother kneels in prayer, as the child feels his imprisonment within her corset. She faints, and is revived with holy water. The moment of life which had drawn so close to the unborn poet, recedes; the lights go out in the church; the chandelier takes on a terrifying resemblance to a gallows. So the poet writes his autobiography, five empty houses marking the stages of his life; the sixth, towards which he moves like a sleep-walker, is the grave. Behind him lie the five episodes of his love, each woman a nail driven into his flesh. By return to the grave, which so much resembles the womb, the circle of life is complete.

The cult of death which gripped Czech poetry suited well the style of Nezval with his unrestrained gift of fantasy: there is something very familiar in his poetic world, of skies split by rainbow and lightning, storms of passion marred by terror and guilt. In his pages we are back in the romantic waste land; it is in some ways as escapist as a visit to the chamber of horrors on a summer holiday—an enjoyable bout of fright from which the reader emerges to breathe the fresh air of day with enhanced pleasure. If one compares the poems of Nezval with those of Závada, whose book *Siréna* (*The Siren*) was published in 1932, there are superficial resemblances; but the mood is basically different. The world of Závada's art is literally God-forsaken; peopled solely by devils and ugliness, a barren land of malice and despair, entirely unrelieved by hope or grace. Mankind is the victim, not of morbid fantasies, but of a gangrene which has eaten into body and soul; it is a procession of cripples and ghosts, handed to the mercies of a devil who lacks all trace of the nobility with which literature has endowed Satan. The implication of Závada's poetry is that there is no hope, no salvation; the poetic escapism which he practises is escape to total despair, symbolized by the unrelieved ugliness with which the poet identifies himself.

The horrific themes of Czech poetry were the subject of much discussion among critics at the time. It was interpreted as a trend towards increasing unreality in literature, and it was the poetists who came in for much of the blame. By their resistance to politically-committed verse in the twenties they had helped the cause of autonomy in art; but in the long run their influence had narrowed its basis and enervated its vigour. Gradually losing contact with the real world, art had become a private adventure of the senses and imagination, a shrine for the small circle of the initiated; and finally a nirvana which had assumed the qualities of a graveyard. While Europe was passing through a phase of social and political convulsions, Czech literature, harping on its favourite themes of transience, decay, and despair, had retreated to a padded cell wherein it could contemplate its own spiritual sickness.

Halas, who no doubt felt himself a prime target of the criticism, replied in defence of current trends. In his view, modern poetry represented not an escape from, but an instinctive reaction to, the contemporary atmosphere of crisis: a sick man scratches his scars, not to impress an audience but to gain relief for himself. Despair was a natural mood for a poet, especially today; the poets' obsession with death was not a rejection of life, but an expression of their will to live, and of their hatred of all that stopped them living as man should. Contemporary poetry was not nihilistic, it sought for a way out of the crisis by the only means open to it—by exploiting the possibilities of its own art; it plunged to the bottom of the well to seek the star that would save it.

One point on which the poets and their critics agreed was that Czech literature was going through a period of crisis which was in some way connected with the crisis in political and social life. The effect of crisis on the writers was varied: in some cases there was a trend towards total irrationalism; poetry confined itself to the realms of the instincts, and gloried in exposing still further the darker sides of man's thoughts and feelings. At the opposite extreme were those few writers who struggled for a neo-realism based on an ideological line dictated by a political cadre. In between lay those who rejected the diabolism of the one group, and the revolutionary orthodoxy of the other. The salient feature of their work was a search for harmony, even in the middle of discord; and gradually they attracted to their camp even those who, like Nezval, expressed in their work a sense of disintegration, corresponding to the neurotic atmosphere of a Europe now heading rapidly for destruction.

7

INTERVAL FOR SURREALISM

AMID the catalogue of gloom and defiance which marks the poetry of the early thirties it is refreshing to come upon two books of verse written as if in holiday spirit from the prevailing atmosphere. They are *Jablko z klína* (*An Apple from the Lap*) by Seifert (1933), and *Sbohem a šáteček* (*A Farewell—a Handkerchief*) by Nezval (1934). In a broadcast talk at the time Seifert revealed his own attitude to his past work: he declared the youthful phase of his poetry to be at an end, and renounced both the revolutionary enthusiasm of his early days, and also the subsequent phase of artistic iconoclasm—which is how he now viewed poetism. His declared aim was no longer to strike the word 'art' from the dictionary and replace it with literary technology, but, in humbler strain, to strive to become a good artist. It was the principle of *continuity* in literature which Seifert now stressed, in common with an increasing number of his contemporaries. This he conceived as in no way a reactionary aim: the idea was not simply to turn back the clock, but to purge his work of merely destructive and superficial elements. To use the jargon of the time, his aim was to set poetry free from artistic athleticism.

The result was poetry of a grace that modern Czech literature had rarely seen, poetry free from moral conflict, social unease, and ideological attachment. All the quaint tricks and verbal pyrotechnics disappeared from Seifert's work. Traditional in form, his verses were simple in expression; their language was so close to vernacular speech that at times it verges on the banal, almost the comic. He had learned to take great risks with language—to walk the tightrope from which one slip was a disaster. Thematically his poetry still embraced the graveyard, but it was without horror—a place for bees to swarm, or lovers to meet. Love, as the most real and delightful of all human experiences, had become the commonest theme of his verses. Far-fetched symbolism, ecstasy, and vertigo were entirely foreign to his poems, of which the prevailing mood was harmonious tranquillity, with more than a touch

of resignation. With theme, style, and mood so classically simple, it is
surprising how great is the impact of his poetry. In fact, poems like
'Image in Water' have immense charm: the poem 'Midnight' catches
with unerring touch the breathless silence of lovers lurking in darkened
doorways. More strange and romantic is the atmosphere of the poem
'The Wax Candle':

> She came from the rustling beehives,
> from the scented flowers' store:
> the sister of the honey,
> washed by its stream, before
>
> she was lifted by angel fingers
> from out of that fragrant spring
> and, at the month of loving,
> bees spun her covering.
>
> When a man, as though yet sleeping,
> before her feet lies dead
> on her train of gloomy shadows,
> she parts her long-tressed head
>
> and down from her waxen body
> a tear falls scaldingly
> 'The bed is laid, beloved,
> where you will lie with me.'[1]

---

[1] Z šumících úlů přišlá
a z vůně sterých květin
sestřička medu,
v němž koupala se předtím,

než z této vonné lázně
andělské ruce ji zvedly,
v měsíci lásky
včely jí roucho předly.

Když člověk mrtev k nohám
jí padne jako spící
na vlečku černých stínů,
tu rozčísne svou kštici

a po voskovém těle
jí žhavá slza skane:
Pojď' se mnou, mrtvý milý,
lůžko je rozestlané.

While Seifert was perfecting the style of personal lyric which is his strongest claim to literary survival, Nezval was on his travels in France, that Mecca of the poetists. His new book was a poetic travelogue, covering a journey from Prague to Vienna and across the Alps to Paris, then via the Mediterranean coast to Italy and home. It is a diary of queer, grotesque, and paradoxical impressions. The world of Nezval's travels, at times like a series of gay or comic picture-postcards, has been aptly compared to scenery reflected in distorting mirrors. In Venice the poet's eye lights on golden coffins gliding on canals, children playing with spiders, and houses like two-decked boats with funnels reversed. He was enchanted with the primitive squalor of the Mediterranean lands, and his hymn of praise of the sea reads like the parody of a classical lyric. It is typical of Nezval that instead of describing a scene he isolates details, and uses them as a spring-board for his own imagination, as though the external world were merely the raw material for poetic fantasy. Delighting in the unexpected, he loves to combine dissimilar elements to form pictorial compositions of a freakish nature. In 'Roofs of Marseilles' his eye draws together two objects—the fine, functional lines of the transborder railway line, and an old woman on a flower-decked balcony, as she sheds grotesque tears for an unfeeling lover:

> Old woman, forget all your dreams of a lover,
> and at last let my train, long delayed, now go by!
> Know that once any love, like a plaything, is broken—
> let it go! spoil no longer your sight as you cry!
>
> Poor heart, your dull Sisyphus stone now abandon,
> to love on for ever! Your vigil resign!
> For your heart is not iron, like the horn-plated sea crabs,
> like the anchors of steel, like the transborder line.[1]

---

[1] Zapomeň stará ženo na miláčka
a nechej přejet zpožděný můj vlak
Věř když se láska poláme jak hračka
je lépe nechat ji a nekazit si pláčem zrak

Ach srdce nech tu Sysifovu práci
milovat na věky a hleď' si jiných her
Vždyť' nejsi z železa jak tito mořští raci
jak tato kotva jak ten transbordér

The poems range from burlesques to snatches of macabre impressionism. Here is a glimpse from the section entitled 'Aquarium':

> Jointed fingers seek the killer
> Conscious guilt remorseful roams
> stretching out to walls and touching
> sleeping children touching homes[1]

The final section of the collection relapses into childish trochees with the return of the poet to the homely scenery of his childhood. Last comes the title poem, ending on a note of uncomplicated nostalgia. As usual, the reader is left wondering whether he is to smile, or not.

Seifert and Nezval had travelled far from the rhetoric and primitivism of their early days; poetry had become in their hands a finely tuned instrument, able to produce effects not possible in prose. Although Seifert had renounced poetism as a style, in one sense his work was now a climax of that movement. The world of his art was in no real sense a reflection of the natural world, but a world with its own laws—its odd juxtapositions and capricious composition was a reflection of the artist. Stripped of all non-poetic accretions, poetry was master in its own house.

So-called 'pure' poetry, in the style of Mallarmé, Valéry, and Rilke, was familiar to Czech readers through translation, and there were few poets of the time who were not influenced by it. Seifert, Halas, Zahradníček, and the younger poets particularly fell under its spell. But in the Czech literary environment each movement of poetry away from the 'real' world met with a corresponding reaction in the reverse direction. The tension is especially marked in the case of the older poets. It is interesting to note its effect on the work of Hora at this time. In 1933-4 he published two books of verse entitled *Tonoucí stíny* (*Drowning Shadows*), and *Dvě minuty ticha* (*Two Minutes Silence*). The titles give some indication of the themes of the poems. The first of the collections seemed to presage a move away from Hora's own metaphysical tack, and incorporated a series of realist social ballads in the style of Wolker. But the heart of the book was a cycle of short lyrics whose elusive nature

---

[1] Články prstů hledají vraha
Tato výčitka svědomí
bloudí a na stěny sahá
sahá na spící děti a na domy

is indicated by some of the titles—'In Solitude', 'From the Dark', 'Over Faust', 'The Milky Way', 'Fading', 'Faraway', 'The Parting Day'. Death and decay had their place in Hora's poetry, but without the overtones of horror and guilt familiar to readers of Halas or Závada. The passage of time was still a theme which fascinated Hora—no longer time as an ingredient in eternity, but time as a road that leads to death. The prevailing mood was resigned and melancholy: the drums and trumpets of social rebellion had disappeared for ever from his work. It is poetry of an intellectual and philosophical kind; classic in its restraint and mastery of literary technique, but without excitement or surprises. Hora had now adopted a theme familiar in classical literature, that of the immortality of art:

> A fleeting pang, your lips' reproach
> live on through the sound of the poet's silver bells.
> All things decay. The image only never fades . . .[1]

The inexorable passage of time condemns man and all his works to decay; over art alone death has no power. The painter and the poet grow old, but the picture and the poem remain as young as on the day of creation. One thinks of the Horatian ode, *'exegi monumentum aere perennius'*, or of Callimachus' memorial for Heracleitus; but the classical poet invoked by Hora is in fact Ovid. The lovely women of Rome were at once his inspiration and the cause of his damnation. In exile he lost all that he valued in life; yet in poetry his passoin is preserved forever.

The title poem of the collection *Two Minutes Silence* is concerned with an actual happening of the time—a mine accident. The occasion affords Hora an opening for an expression of total despair equalling anything in Závada or Halas. The cry of human distress typified by the mine disaster is a link between life and the artist, fenced off by his intellect, and condemned to a barren labyrinth. The poet seeks escape from his isolation by contact not only with the tribulations of ordinary life, but also, more romantically, with the spirit of the past. He invokes the ancestors who, being dead, are in spirit still among us. He sees them rise from the surface of his native stream: once flesh and blood like himself, they are now the shadows of a misty past that cannot

---

[1] Minuta žalu, žaloba tvých úst
zní stříbrem zvonů z vůle básníkovy.
Vše pomine. Jen obraz zůstává . . .

relieve his isolation. The poet dismisses the ghosts that are his link backwards in time. Death alone is the companion who waits to welcome him to the prepared home:

> Shadows of receding shadows
> fly to your eternal homeland!
> Flow along the starry mainstream
> marshalled in death's harmony.
> Trembling with the heaven's passing
> now I live, and now I perish
> I, the flower in rain—the floodgate
> setting in God's hand my lifeblood
> when his bidding comes to me.[1]

The neo-baroque atmosphere of Hora's later verse links him with his younger contemporary Halas, whose new book, *Hořec* (*The Gentian*), was first published in 1933. In style he has been described as the poet of intensity rather than extensity: by concentration on one chord or one detail, he would extract from it the maximum effect. In one sense he was at the opposite pole to Nezval, and in comparing the two poets Šalda once selected two poems of similar theme—Nezval's 'Six Empty Houses' and Halas' 'Before the Return'—to show an essential difference in their method. Both poems deal with man's desire to find security by return to the mother's womb, that Freudian lost paradise. For Nezval the theme serves merely as a starting point for a mass of childhood memories and adult fantasy, a chain reaction of impressions, like a stone thrown into water and producing ever-widening circles. Halas, by contrast, emphasizes the severance of the umbilical chord that cut him off from the womb's living darkness. Cast out and isolated, he expresses his will to regain the lost refuge by physical concentration, as in sleep his body assumes the huddled posture of the unborn child:

---

[1] Odejděte, stíny stínů,
ve věčnou svou domovinu!
Vplyňte v proud a v mléčnou dráhu,
stíny, smrti smířené!
Já se chvěji v nebes tahu,
já teď žiju, já teď hynu,
já, květ v dešti, splav, jenž složí
pěnu krve své v dlaň boží,
až si na mne vzpomene.

> I find peace once more, huddling close
> as I dream amid the quiet heart-beats . . .¹

popular Freudism was evidently part of Halas' stock-in-trade. So too was the theme of art itself: as poetry was to Biebl the wings of Icarus, so to Halas it was the coin in the mouth of the corpse, paying his passage across the river of forgetfulness. But the poet professes a lack of faith even in the power of art. His paradoxical rejection of poetry is expressed in the final poem of the collection *Parting of the Ways*, a theatrical gesture renouncing personal poetry in favour of participation in the real drama of social revolt. (The sentiment was apparently more than a poetic gesture, for it is confirmed in his personal correspondence of the period.) By participation in the common effort he would overcome the isolation of the artist, but on the outcome of the struggle he has no illusions:

> in this dim age of indecision
> our lives in words too often yet we spend
>
> If only could come crashing down in thunder
> the grief of masses piled up to the stars
> and all my hapless race lie buried under²

Love poems, where nostalgia replaces extinction, afford Halas an occasional opportunity to relapse into the graceful and melodious style of which he was capable; in contrast to the poems of Seifert, it is the passing, not the presence of love, that is emphasized:

> Steps that recede in the distance
> who passed that way?
> how much we loved you
> who can say?

---

¹ klid nalézám zas v schoulení
kde v snění jen srdce tiše bije . . .

² Translated by E. Osers and J. K. Montgomery:
v tomto věku který se nerozhoduje
utráceli jsme život v nich vždy znova

Kéž zřítí se již dolů s rachotem
žal zástupů až k hvězdám navršený
a zasype rod smutných k němuž patřil jsem

(From the collection *The Face*)

Maybe the feet of the women
loving and loved by me
tremble yet never discover
which could it be

Passing and never returning
as well she passed on
yet yearning still lingers
when love is gone

Steps that recede in the distance
who passed that way?
maybe we loved you still . . .
fading fading away.[1]

Halas was as distrustful of formal excellence as he was of everything else, and even in this book we find traces of the broken syntax, half-rhymes, and discords which are a feature of his style. But it is still perhaps the most attractive and poetic of his books, containing some of his best personal poetry. The first edition of the book was illustrated by the surrealist painter Toyen with three brilliant lithographs which emphasized the romantic quality of the work.

Halas was at the time under fire from many quarters. Conservative critics were impatient with his graveyard flowers and his anti-lyricism; they accused him of cynical posing, of superficiality, and of monotony. Nezval deplored his abandonment of poetism; Šalda, while welcoming

---

[1] Tichnoucí kroky v dáli
komu patříte
jak jsme vás milovali
vy to nevíte

Patříte ženám snad
co měly rády nás
chvět se a nepoznat
která teď' přešla z vás

Přešla a víc se nevrátí
dobře že minula
toužení nezkrátí
když láska zhynula

Tichnoucí kroky v dáli
komu patříte
snad jsme vás milovali
míjíte mizíte

his verse as a triumph of neo-baroque, warned against the danger of monotony and sentimentality. But the sharpest criticism came from the self-styled progressives. From 1934 Halas was editing the literary journal *Rozhledy* on which he co-operated with a group of Catholic writers, who were his close friends. The association brought him under suspicion with the hard-line left-wingers, and the quarrel soon came into the open. Halas and Závada had taken part in the preparation of an unsigned article which opened a frontal attack on Wolker, on the occasion of the tenth anniversary of his death. Wolker, as the only consistently successful protagonist of Proletarian literature, had become a symbol of social commitment in art. The attempt to give Czech literature a greater social orientation in the thirties was partly a result of the Moscow Rappists' conference, and the general aim was supported even by writers like Nezval, who rejected the point of view of the Rappists. But in spite of their rather half-hearted support, the campaign was without any real success, and its failure was a sore point with the leftists. Although Halas overtly associated himself with their social views, he was accused of deserting the ranks, to attack a socialist poet in the interest of Catholic reaction.

The wild charges and counter-insults which flew across the literary arena in the thirties seem often intended not to be taken seriously, and the poets and their critics remained personal friends. But they illustrate the tensions which enveloped literary life at the time. Within the avantgarde the struggle resolved itself into one between the advocates of socially committed art, and those who seemed to have retired to an ivory tower. The real strength and appeal of the latter group can be seen from their influence on the younger generation, from whose ranks two poets of exceptional promise, F. Hrubín and V. Holan, had recently gained notice. In 1933 Hrubín published the collection *Zpíváno z dálky* (*Sung from Far Away*): he had the unusual distinction of seeing his first book reviewed by Šalda, who characterized his poetry as unspoilt, abstract, ecstatic, melodious, ultra-violet in tone and colour, full of subtle suggestions of life and premonitions of death. The other new celebrity, who had in fact been publishing verse since 1926, was Vladimír Holan, whose earlier work, *Triumf smrti* (*Triumph of Death*), by its title gives some suggestion of the author's bent. So Holan began a long literary career which was to establish him as a great figure in modern Czech literature, and as one of its greatest enigmas. His books *Vanutí* (*Breezes*) and *Oblouk* (*The Arch*) were first published in 1932 and 1934. The phantoms of phantoms, and

abstractions of abstractions, which haunt his verse, have given Holan
the reputation of being among the 'purest' and most withdrawn of
Czech poets. Each poem is a structure of ideas; its content a complex
series of inter-relationships. The breezes are those which waft the poet,
without conscious will or thought, into the dark recesses of Being—he
is a sleep-walker in a mysterious land. Somewhere in the unfathomable
distance is the quest for which he must pass right through the facade
of life. For a moment the curtain trembles, admitting a suggestion of
the forbidden secret ('The Cry of the Symbols'). Holan's poetry is the
antithesis of the Wolker tradition which set the eye and the emotions
at the centre of art. Beside the intellectual distillations of Holan,
Wolker seems almost journalese and immature. But an art so finely
wrought as to lose all the grossness and distress of life is in danger of
losing its vital humus. Wolker's poetry, technically inferior as it may
be, has the life and appeal that the pure poets lack. Holan wrote in
riddles, and the breakdown of understanding between himself and the
reader has always restricted his popularity. Like Halas, Holan used his
mastery of technique to vary his graceful style with deformed syntax,
crude rhymes, and grotesque word forms.

While the advocates of a socialist, or at least a realist, literature con-
fronted the poets of flawless abstraction, Nezval found himself in a
rather peculiar position. Outwardly and vociferously he was for the
realists, but in the whole spirit of his work he was much closer to the
pure poetry of Halas and Holan. In this dilemma he followed his
normal individualist bent by accepting neither position, and criticizing
both. In his own work, however, to an increasing degree he gave a free
rein to his fantasy, writing in a style which claimed to be more realistic
than realism. His new love was Surrealism, which sought to relate art
to life by deciphering the secrets of man's subconscious mind. The
French surrealists, to whose movement Nezval now pledged his en-
thusiastic adherence, had rejected all forms of mysticism in literature,
and had combined their bizarre literary efforts with a militantly left-
wing attitude in politics. During his recent visit to France Nezval had
come into personal contact with their leaders, and had helped to translate into Czech the poems of Paul Eluard and André Breton.

Historically, the movement they led had its inauspicious beginnings
in Dada, the anti-art and anti-logic movement of the early twenties,
which had, as we have seen, influenced the young poetists. Abroad,
Dadaism had not lasted very long, but after the disintegration of the
movement some of its more serious-minded adherents had carried their

interest in psycho-analysis into the realm of literature and painting. Breton had worked during the war as a doctor in a military hospital, and there he had come into contact with patients whose mental balance had been disturbed by war experiences. He had applied to literary composition the methods of psycho-analysis, believing that extraordinary compositions, resembling those of great poets, could emerge from a mind whose inner censor had been stilled by derangement, and that similar effects could be produced by allowing the subconscious to take over while in the act of composing. Breton was especially interested in the creations and self-expression of people in abnormal states—subjects not inhibited by conventional taboos, conventions, or given styles of behaviour. The art-forms of children, the ravings of lunatics, and the self-expression of men under the influence of drugs or hypnosis formed a part of his study. But the richest source of material came from dreams: many surrealist poems claimed to be automatic texts, transcribed immediately upon waking, and unbounded by canons of logic, judgcmcnt, or taste.

Poetism had clearly owed a good deal to the surrealists, and it could be argued that Nezval's 'Amazing Magician', written at the beginning of his career, had many features of a surrealist poem. But the theoretical work of the poetists, especially of Teige, had led them away from surrealist theory. To Teige, who had approached literature with many of the criteria of architecture or the film, the impact of a poem depended primarily on its sensuous evocation. Just as beauty in the plastic arts depended on a combination of colour, shape, light, and shade, so in literature it depended on a complex relationship of sound, together with such suggestions of colour, taste, form, etc., as its words could evoke. The interpretation of poetry as pure sound had appealed to Nezval, who came to literature from music. Had the poetists carried to its logical conclusion this part of their theory, their poems might have become experiments in phonetics and acoustics, aided by typography. In renouncing poetism Seifert had declared himself weary of such verbal acrobatics, and in this he was perhaps echoing a general feeling that content had been sacrified to style. But in any case the essential assumptions of Teige's theory were challenged by the budding psychoanalysts, who pointed out that optical perception did not entirely depend on the eye, nor literary perception on the ear. The effect of a poem depended upon the reactions of the audience—reactions limited by its receptivity, imagination, sympathies, understanding, and mental background. Colour, shape and sound had no *particular* emotive appeal: their appeal lay in their psychological associations. The proper study for the poet was not the natural scenery, but the human mind. Thus Nezval, in the last stages of the poetist movement, was led back to the study of poetry via the psychologist's laboratory. Drawing his material from the subterranean corridors of his own mind, he sought to evoke an echo in the subconscious mind of the audience, who would respond, without consciously understanding why. Such poetry although strange and often incomprehensible, was the reverse of abstract. It was described as psychic materialism, because it took as its province not only the whole world known to man in his waking state, but also the lost, buried world of dreams and hallucinations. Surrealism claimed to be realism plus—a super-realist form of art.

The surrealist group of Prague, founded by Nezval, included painters and musicians, but apart from Nezval, Biebl alone of the poets showed real interest. Czech surrealist poetry is almost entirely identified with the work of Nezval himself; in particular with his three collections of verse, *Žena v množném čísle* (*Woman in the Plural*), *Praha s prsty deště* (*Prague with Fingers of Rain*), and *Absolutní Hrobař* (*The Unadulterated Sexton*).

The French surrealist poets had abandoned all 'artificial' poetic devices, such as rhyme, which limit the free movement of the imagination. Nezval was more cautious, using rhyme still, but in a ding-dong fashion reminiscent of the nursery rhyme. In reviewing his work, a contemporary critic in fact slipped among Nezval's couplets one taken from an old book of children's rhymes, and demonstrated that the effect was indistinguishable from that of modern surrealist verse. In general, however, Nezval's poetry was not of this character. The structure of the verses was very free, but the effect was certainly that of poetry rather than of prose. In many poems a rhythmical pattern was set up not by a regular number of syllables to the line, nor by a regular accentual pattern, but by the repetition of a sound, word, or phrase at the beginning of each line. His technique thus substituted initial-markers for end-markers in the structure of the poem—a device which gave greater freedom, and produced a mildly hypnotic effect, but was basically no less 'artificial' that the traditional end-rhymes. The best of Nezval's surrealist poems are in fact the result of his experiments in technique; there is no sign of an *abandonment* of technique, and the texts, although spontaneously flowing, hardly pretend to be automatic. There are times when style and content match very well, as in his 'Song of Songs'. Here the hypnotic repetition of formulae in the style of the Old Testament litany provides a vehicle for the modern poet's enumeration and adoration of woman's every amorous feature.

One advantage claimed for surrealist poetry was that its methods of free composition threw up fresh combinations of objects and ideas— 'Beautiful as the accidental meeting of an umbrella and a sewing machine upon an operating table', as Nezval once quoted. The linking of objects between which there is no logical connection is an experience common in dreams, and in much surrealist verse the combination often veils sexual symbolism. In style, Nezval himself used as a conscious working principle the device of startling juxtapositions in order to achieve a novelty of impact:

When words were new they shone next to each other in their unceasing, native intensity. Gradually from their frequent usage was evolved phraseology. . . . If one is to evoke their original impact, it is necessary to break down set phrases. Logic is precisely that which makes of shining words mere phrases. Logically the glass belongs to the table, the star to the sky, the door to the staircase. That is why they go unnoticed. It was necessary to set the star to the table; the glass hard by the piano and the angels; the door next to the ocean. The idea was to unveil reality; to give back its shining image, as on the first day of its existence. If I did this at the expense of logic, it was an attempt at realism raised to a higher degree.[1]

Probably Nezval's most successful surrealist collection was *Prague with Fingers of Rain*. The old city, still very much alive, but containing within itself the relics and associations of fifty generations, was a happy subject for a poet who delighted in bizarre juxtapositions. Of his subject Nezval wrote:

I felt that you, the city of a hundred spires, still half-submerged in old legends, and wearing before our eyes an enchanted robe spun from Spring's lights, you could place all your old magic and youthful uncertainty in the service of the poetry we love. Thus I learned to love you; to call your bridges and streets by their true names; to evoke from them something of their true spell. My subjective life . . . tried to make of you a stage for my yearning, and a lexicon to express the colour of our days, the colour of our frenzied loves, our desires.[2]

---

[1] 'The Ink-drop', first published in the journal *ReD*, vol. 1, no. 9.
[2] Introduction to the second edition of *Most*.

H

In recalling the composition of the book Nezval typically fishes his words from the strange waters in which lay his verse of the time. The poems are for the most part highly finished. Repetition without monotony is still a feature of his style:

> It is noon:
> Prague is sleeping and yet awake, like a fantastic dragon,
> Like a sacred rhinoceros whose cage is the sky,
> Like a stalactite organ playing softly,
> Like a symbol of resurrection and of treasures from dried-up lakes,
> Like an army in panoply saluting the emperor,
> Like an army in panoply saluting the sun,
> Like an army in panoply turned into jasper.[1]

At times one seems to be reading not a surrealist poem so much as the evocation of a surrealist painting:

> Like berets thrown into the air,
> Berets of boys, cocottes and cardinals,
> Turned into stone by the sorcerer Zito
> At the great feast;
> Berets with Chinese lanterns
> On the eve of St. John's Day
> When fireworks are let off—
> Yet also like a town of umbrellas opened skyward as shields against rockets:
> All this is Prague.[2]

Translated by E. Osers:

[1] Je poledne
Praha bdí v polosnu tak jako fantastický drak
Jak posvátný nosorožec jehož klecí je nebe
Jak krápníkové varhany jejichž píšťaly zpívají
Jak symbol zmrtvýchvstání a pokladů vyschlých jezer
Jak armáda v těžkém brnění když zdraví císaře
Jak armáda v těžkém brnění když pozdravuje slunce
Jak armáda v těžkém brnění zakletá v jaspisu

[2] Jak čapky vyhozené do výše
Jak čapky dětí kokot a kardinálů
Jež zaklel kouzelník Žito
O veliké slavnosti
Jak čapky s lampiony
Vpředvečer svatého Jana

Nezval, who knew Prague so well, felt himself at times inoculated against her strangeness and poetry; his book conveys the attempt to break down this familiarity. He is like a person who sees a familiar view through new eyes by looking at it backwards, between his legs, and upside-down. The resulting giddiness is part of the effect. The glimpses of the real city which appear, have this in common that they convey the impressions of one who sees it for the first time—a bewildering jumble of objects which set off diversely progressing streams of associations. It is a pity that Nezval saw fit to include in this strange and attractive book a section of so-called social poems, containing some mechanical attacks on the capitalist system. His inclusion of these tired didactic verses within a collection of imaginative lyrics seems like a concession to the social-realists, and an attempt to hold together the latter with the avantgardists in one progressive front.

The reception for Nezval's latest efforts was less than cordial. Traditionalist critics received his more bizarre work with icy disapproval, while the politically committed writers regarded him as an anarchist. When Nezval protested innocently that surrealism had a positive revolutionary role—that it was an expression of defiance against a corrupt order—there were few who took him seriously. His poems, even when praised for their lyrical quality, were criticized as a mere exploitation of unbridled fantasy, lacking any confrontation with reality, an eruption of dreams and hallucinations transposed into poetry. In so far as a surrealist poem was genuinely spontaneous and uncontrolled, it was not a work of art, but a mere 'happening'. From the Marxist camp on the other hand, Nezval's poetry was described as a psychological laxative, whose only social value was therapeutic, to free his readers from their own repressions. As far as the surrealists' political stance was concerned, it was regarded as a mere theatrical gesture, in no way connected with their artistic programme.

Within the circle of his friends, Nezval was criticized for splitting the already thin ranks of the avantgarde by his formation of the Prague surrealist group. He was genuinely concerned about the rift, and as an expression of solidarity with the leftists, he agreed to join the Czech

---

Když se pálí ohně
A také jak město deštníků rozevřených na ochranu proti raketám
To vše je Praha

H*

delegation to the Congress of Soviet writers held at Moscow in August 1934. In spite of his Communist views Nezval, like many Czech writers, had many reservations about literary life in the U.S.S.R., and these had been increased by the dogmatic theses propounded at the Kharkov conference four years before. Meanwhile, however, the situation in Russia was said to have changed. The Rappist movement had been disbanded, and its leader had disappeared from Soviet literary life. Prague literary journals had carried news of a new Russian campaign for a return to the classics, and of the new doctrine of 'socialist realism'. Before leaving for Moscow Nezval announced that he intended to defend the surrealist position at the conference, and to help broaden the front of progressive writers.

The conference was primarily and officially one of Soviet writers; but its significance was expanded by the presence of foreign delegates and by the ominous international situation. The smell of the book-burnings in Nazi Germany was felt even in the Moscow Hall of Columns, as Ilya Ehrenburg has written; and the congress became a political demonstration of anti-Fascist solidarity. The Russians were looking for allies in Western Europe, and the presence of French and Czech observers appeared as a hopeful sign. The Soviet literary spokesmen seemed to have abandoned their dogmatic position; and there were many indications that at last a common front might be formed between liberal and left-wing writers all over Europe.

The writer's right to be obscure and eccentric was defended by Ehrenburg, who ridiculed the Soviet practice of publishing a red list and a black list of writers, and calling it literary criticism. Bukharin, who had for several years been in the wilderness for political errors, made a dashing speech in which he dismissed 'declarative' verse as unworthy of the name of poetry, and called for literary diversity within a common front. He spoke of socialist realism, and in his interpretation it seemed to be an upgrading of classical realism, but including the best of modern avantgarde art. On the other hand, and in more ominous terms, Zhdanov described it as 'truthfulness and historical correctness of artistic description, combined with the task of ideological transformation in the spirit of socialism'.

Not abashed by such stern prescriptions, Nezval vigorously defended the surrealist position. He claimed that poetic thought, once held to be miraculous, is based on emotions which can be analyzed and explained. Poetry was the *adaptation of reality by fantasy* using the tools of dramatization, condensation, and substitution. Signs and symbols in dreams could be traced to instincts restrained by the mind-censor, and appearing in symbolic form. Surrealism was a synthesis of reality and fantasy, discipline and freedom. The surrealists, like their Soviet colleagues, were against formalism, against naturalism, and against the idealism of 'pure' poetry. They had always made clear their opposition to Fascism, and their adherence to the world socialist movement.

Nezval believed that by his explanations he had cleared up many misunderstandings and hoped that his visit heralded an era of co-operation on the literary front. But he was acute enough to see that the liberal views of Bukharin, Ehrenburg, and Pasternak were not shared by the Soviet literary establishment. Nezval found with dismay that his remarks were misrepresented in the Soviet press, and his long defence of surrealism was totally omitted from the report on the conference. In a survey of international literary trends, Radek did not bother even to mention left-wing literature outside the U.S.S.R.

One positive result of the Moscow congress was a decision on the part of the delegates to meet again in Paris during the following year. The conference was in fact held, amid the hopeful atmosphere of the French Popular Front. Co-operation between the writers of East and West Europe seemed to be assured, and the delegates included such diverse characters as Gide, Brecht, Huxley, Aragon, Pasternak, Forster, and Brod. But a chilling note was struck when Nezval, who wished again to put the surrealist view, could not get a hearing, and Breton was expelled from the conference.

In Prague the attempt to draw together the left-wing writers continued, and a new journal *Blok* was launched to give the movement a new platform. But the attempt at unity was a failure. Nezval and Teige found themselves labelled as counter-revolutionaries and idealistic acrobats; wild charges were made, identifying surrealism with Fascism. Hopes that Russian literature was turning back to its earlier experimental phase proved to be quite unfounded; and news began to reach Prague of the Russian purges involving well-known Soviet writers, including Bukharin himself. As the news of literary activities in Russia became more depressing, so the Czech Communist critics became more rigid in their attitude, violently condemning any criticism of the U.S.S.R. It became clear that the hoped-for co-operation between Marxist and experimental art was doomed. The following choice comment, from the pen of the once liberal Marxist S. K. Neumann, is indicative of the literary atmosphere of Prague:

It is now quite clear to me that the so-called avantgarde—at least in literature and painting—with its play on intuition, with its uncontrollable and often feigned super-realism, with its freudism and cult of the sub-conscious, with its belief that 'free play' is a higher form of literary production than purposeful, logical composition, is the direct descendant of the so-called idealistic world attitude, and the recognizably bastard offspring of bourgeois decadence. Their sterile efforts to become the bedfellow of the avantgarde of social revolution, which recognizes one method and one truth—dialectical materialism—is an irresponsible farce.

The broad front of left-wing artists which had, ten years earlier, included such a motley array of individualists and eccentrics, had now narrowed to the limits of a political cadre. Hora and Seifert had long since left the fold; Halas and Závada were now, in the spirit of their work, much closer to the Catholics and the abstract poets. Nezval and Biebl alone hung on, striving to heal the breach between the 'realists' and the experimentalists. The end came finally in 1938 when, after a stormy meeting at which Nezval and Teige quarrelled bitterly, the Czech surrealist group was dissolved. The socialist realists had won their sterile victory by proclaiming as the friends of Fascism all who could not, or would not, accept their literary doctrines. In this grim atmosphere avantgarde art, with all its wild pretensions and bizarre overtones, seemed already like a historical curiosity, outdated by the ruthless march of events, of which Czechoslovakia was soon to be the tragic centre.

8
PUT OUT THE LIGHTS!

THE brave words of rebellion which in 1919 had been a central theme of poetry, had now, less than twenty years later, either disappeared from the poet's repertoire or had changed their meaning. The literature of revolution had acquired its own quaint brand of orthodoxy, with criteria drawn from the officially propagated style of socialist realism. Poets like Neumann, Nezval, and Halas were still writing 'socialist' poems, and younger writers like Taufer and Noha followed their lead. But the declamatory and programmatic nature of such work robbed it of real interest: its conformity to the new models cut it off from the genuine revolutionary tradition which recognized no master except conscience, and no orthodoxy except the unorthodox. On the international scene it was André Gide who raised his voice against the literary trend of the socialist camp, and reasserted the view of the poet as the eternal rebel.

The poetry of the twenties had thrived on experiment and upon the rejection of authority—literary, political, or ideological. In art, as a Czech theoretician once remarked, 'the norm is the breaking of the norm'. By the late thirties the old rebellious spirit was no longer typical of Czech imaginative literature, though its after-effects still lingered on. They were to be seen still in the anti-art, anti-logic, and anti-tradition poems of the surrealists, appealing not to the intellect or even to the feelings, but to the irrational. The cult of the primitive, and the dethronement of reason in art, is a feature of one brand of European literature between the wars, corresponding as it does in politics, to the breakdown of faith in ordered government, and the dethronement of democracy. In 1937 Nezval published an interesting anthology of modern European poetry, *Moderní Básnické Směry* (*Trends in Modern Poetry*), arranged to show an ordered development from nineteenth-century symbolism, through Futurism and Constructivism to Dada and Surrealism. It was in the latter than Nezval saw the culmination of modern European art, an art liberated from logic, stemming from the borderland of the human mind, and aptly reflecting the neurotic tempo of the modern world. It is worth noting that the trend to anarchy and neo-primitivism was not confined to the surrealists. Stylistically it appeared in the broken syntax, the grotesque juxtapositions, the ugly half-rhymes, and the strange coinages of poets who did not write in the surrealist style, Závada, Halas, and Holan.

At first sight it seems a self-contradiction to couple together the work of Nezval, with its appeal to sub-emotion, with the 'pure' poetry that was an elaborate network of intellectual forms. But each, in its own way, was expressing a similar reaction to the contemporary scene: each was, in effect, a literature of withdrawal and escape. In the collection *Dokořán* (*Wide Open*) Halas expressed very clearly the feeling of helpless disengagement, picturing himself as swept away by the dark, underground rivers of the imagination. Of similar tone were the latest poems of Biebl. After years of silence he had returned to publication with *Zrcadlo noci* (*Mirror to the Night*), a collection including love poems, some reminiscences of the now-distant First World War, and a surrealist cycle. Biebl's poems were as strange and exotic as ever: surrealist fantasy now supplied the escape route previously afforded by distant vistas and tropical jungles. Only in the love poems did he give an impression of personal involvement, and his most attractive verse is still in the style which he had long made his own:

> She had long sea-lashes sweeping,
> And from Kotor's land she sailed,
> Still her eyelids haunt me, sleeping
> Still I see her eyes unveiled.

> Eyelids like the tall ships swaying,
> Bowls of wine that glimmered brightly,
> Out of far, clear countries straying,
> Where forgetfulness comes lightly.[1]

---

[1] Translated by E. Pargeter:

> Měla dlouhé mořské řasy
> Byla nejspíš z Kotoru
> Její víčka vzpomínám si
> Když je zvedla nahoru
>
> Její víčka pokyv bárek
> Její víčka číše vína
> Pocházela z čirých dálek
> Kde se snadno zapomíná

But escapist fantasies and romantic extravanganzas were in fact no longer typical of modernist Czech poetry. Where fantasy held its ground, it tended to take on an increasingly gloomy aspect—the dreams became nightmares, centring on apocalyptic visions of destruction. Even over Czech surrealist verse, in its later phases, the ominous external situation cast its shadow. Nezval's poem '*Malá Atlantida*' ('Little Atlantis') is a less than serious portrayal of a theme growing only too familiar in imaginative literature—the vision of the waters swirling for ever over the doomed continent.

In a less dramatic form the motif of ruin was carried into a very human setting by Halas in his long poem '*Staré ženy*' ('Aged Women') published in 1935. In form 'Aged Women' closely resembled Nezval's poem 'The Song of Songs'. In the style of a litany it invoked, not without monotony and cruelty, the familiar physical features of woman—not, as in 'The Song of Songs', woman in her hour of beauty and beguilement, but woman sagging in the comfortless twilight of old age. Halas caught his effects by an intense concentration on detail, economy of words, and a calculated use of dissonance, rhythmical irregularity, and word deformities to contrast with the charm of his verse. The formal elements blended well with the theme of the poem—monotony of tone with the drabness of age; verbal deformity with physical ugliness; vernacular speech with the coarseness which no longer hopes to attract admiration:

> dead Sunday afternoons
> made sad by the faces of old women
> faces no longer reflecting life
> only slow death only infirmity
> no remembrance no daydreams
> no desire no hope
> only old age only the sleeping worm
>
> oh faces of aged women
> with the curtain of past hanging so heavily
> lift off the skin and it is Death himself
> oh faces of aged women[1]

---

[1] Translated by E. Osers:

> mrtvá odpoledne nedělní
> smutná tvářemi starých žen
> v nichž nic se již neobráží
> jenom skomírání jenom nemoc

The 1930s saw a great shift of taste in Czech literature, especially in poetry. Ever since 1918 a *leitmotif* had been the liberation of art from tradition, in theme, form, and style. The consequent gain in freedom was a feature of contemporary art; but it was a freedom gained at the expense of order and discipline: Surrealism seems in retrospect to have been the final phase of this movement. The anarchical tendencies of modern art had been consistently opposed by conservative critics like Arne Novák who acted as guardians of tradition, applying to new writing the strictest canons of taste derived from the past. For many years the conflict of views between the protagonists of freedom in art, and those of discipline, had assumed the nature of a confrontation between the generations. But during the thirties, in the camp of the younger (and no longer so young) generation the pendulum began to swing back. At its most superficial level the change is visible in the decline of free verse, the return of punctuation to poetry, and the spectacle of modernist poets like Nezval writing in the classical form of the sonnet and rondel. Artist and public alike were weary of anarchy and gimmickry: the austere defenders of tradition found themselves on common ground with the Marxist critics, who urged a return to the discipline of the party collective.

If there is one feature which marks the poetry of the years preceding the Second World War, it is the movement, in style, theme, and feeling, back to tradition. At the same time personal poetry declines in popularity, and social themes gain new life—above all the theme of national survival. In an atmosphere of secure progress this theme has little appeal in art. It is in the moment of danger that familiar things, which have suddenly become precarious, take on enhanced importance. In the years 1937–9, as war became increasingly likely, the first target for destruction seemed to be the Czech lands, with Prague as their centre. Now, as twenty years before, the feeling of common danger drew attention away from the things which divided people to the things which united them. Traditionally the Czechs had seen themselves as a small Slavic group which owed its very existence in a hostile world to its sense

---

není vzpomínky není zasnění
není toužení ani naděje
jenom stáří jenom červ ještě spící

vy tváře starých žen
s clonou minula tak těžce visící
jen kůži odhrňte a je to smrt
vy tváře starých žen

of solidarity. Through the bad times in the nation's past, when their history had been denigrated, their language persecuted, and their literature burned, the symbol and the cement of their unity were their traditions. Like the ikons of priests they were reverently accepted, preserved, and handed on from one generation to another in the hope of better days. The Czechs' title to nationhood was their language and their past: idealized in legend and romance it was their common source of pride and faith.

So, in their new perils, the poets reacted according to the pattern of the past. Suddenly the themes of cultural continuity and national survival swamped all others in new writing. In their work, modern poets consciously sought to link up with those of a preceding era. Recent styles like Expressionism, Poetism, and Surrealism rapidly disappeared from new writing. Nineteenth-century Czech romanticism and even baroque art once more became centres of intense interest and research. The classic exponent of the village novel, Božena Němcová, took on the dimensions of a literary Joan of Arc: poems were written about her, and dedicated to her memory by modernist writers like Halas and Seifert.

But the most widely acknowledged symbol of Czech poetic tradition was Karel Hynek Mácha, author of the greatest romantic epic in the Czech language. In 1936 the centenary of his death coincided with a great upsurge of nationalist feeling, and the celebrations took on the flavour of a national demonstration. The occasion produced a new literature about the poet, written not only by scholars and critics but also by writers who had all their lives proclaimed their indifference to tradition. Mácha's poetry became a new cult, inspiring a whole series of new poems in his style and memory. Among the most striking tributes was a new book of verse by Hora entitled *Máchovské variace* (*Variations on Mácha*). The book did not set out to be an imitation of the master, but a poetic exposition of Mácha's relevance to Hora's own time. Plunging into the atmosphere of Mácha's poetic world Hora recreated the scenery of the romantic wasteland—the ruins, demonic loves, unmentionable secrets, and the passage of time over the whispers of dead lovers. The mysterious figure of Mácha himself, who died young, becomes symbolic of the secrets snatched away by time before they can be fully decyphered. Time, the destroyer, mocks the promise of the glorious May day that is the opening scene of Mácha's epic. Like the guilty passion of the doomed lovers, the poet's rose must turn to ashes. Only in his dream, converted into art, the rose lives on: thus time is conquered, and the poet's brothers, still unborn, may walk in his steps.

A moment caught by the artist endures for ever in the memory of mankind: for below the level of common life is that other time, encompassing past and future, in which each noble act gains new life and becomes a piece of eternity.

There is an epilogue to the cult of Mácha as the symbol of Czech culture and its survival against odds. When the poet's burial place, at Litoměřice, was occupied by the Germans, the Czech authorities gained permission to exhume the remains, and rebury them in Prague in the old citadel where her traditional heroes are placed. In May 1939 the coffin, wrapped in elaborately woven cloth after the style of the ancient Czech kings, was carried through the streets of Prague amid scenes of mourning, as though the corpse belonged to one personally known by men today. In such style Mácha came back to the home prepared for him, and the return became the theme of many poems: Hora, Seifert, Nezval, and Holan were among those who wrote verses of impressive quality on this occasion, and by their efforts invested old Prague with a new legend.

It was natural that poets should see in literature the symbol of continuity and survival—the thread that held together the dead past and the unknown future. But the common heritage of the people was something wider—the language and the land, with all its associations of myth, legend, and belief. Czechoslovakia was a secular state, and much of its modern literature had been irreligious, if not actively anti-religious. But the pre-war years saw an impressive revival of Catholic literature, which numbered among its contributors even avantgarde writers like Seifert, Závada, and Halas. The greatest exponent of religious verse of the time was almost certainly Jan Zahradníček, who caught the ear of the time with his books *Žíznivé léto* (*The thirsty Summer*) and *Pozdravení slunci* (*Greetings to the Sun*). With these books his poetic world shifts from the mystical half-light of tormented fantasy into bright sunshine where the centre and symbol of peace, order, and security is the poet's homeland. Abandoning the free style of his earlier work, Zahradníček now wrote in verse of strict traditional form, including sonnets, and poems of epic style. His new books were highly rated by Šalda, who rejoiced in their classical harmony, and welcomed in them an artistic feast of light and peace. Combining religious motifs with national tradition Zahradníček set at the very heart of his work a vision of the sunny Czech land redeemed by the faith and hope of her people—at once her sons, her champions, and the heirs to her abundance.

When one compares the poetry of 1936–9 with that written twenty
years earlier, there is a striking difference in the personal attitudes
revealed. In 1918 in the morrow of victory and national vindication,
when one might have expected to find fanfares of triumph, the young
poets were silent. The very success of nationalism in establishing the
new state had robbed it of interest as a motif for contemporary art.
Twenty years later, when the state was about to be destroyed, the land
and its people had become once more a theme of absorbing interest and
common sentiment. What is perhaps more surprising to the Anglo-
Saxon viewer, is that the popular vehicle of shared sentiment was
poetry. An occasion for an outburst of lyric verse was the funeral of
T. G. Masaryk, the president-liberator, in 1937. That autumn day the
muffled drums, the rolling gun-carriage, and the last salutes were felt
with icy foreboding in Prague. Writers as radical as Seifert and Nezval,
who had consistently derided nationalistic pomp, on this occasion
saluted Masaryk's memory by poems published in the popular press.
The response of the man-in-the-street was astonishing; Seifert's
verses were reprinted six times before satisfying popular demand. So,
in this way, and at this late hour, the poetists' gay forecast that the
modern world could dispense with poetry received its final refutation.
And while daily newspapers were boosting their circulations by printing
lyric verse, Hora was adding to his reputation with the monumental
poem '*Zpěv rodné zemi*' ('Song to one's Native Land'), whose theme was
the continuity of blood, language, and tradition of the land, with its
twin recurring symbols of the cradle and the grave.

The intense involvement of poets in a communal experience was not
an unmixed gain. There is a romantic and sentimental tone in many of
the poems written in the period, and their attachment to a particular
situation has dated them. But with all their faults the occasional verses
of the time have a touching effect which has rarely been paralleled in
modern imaginative literature. One such example of poetic journalese
may be quoted. In September 1938, when general mobilization was
proclaimed in Prague and war seemed imminent, the city was suddenly
blacked out by an air-raid warning—abortive, like the mobilization
itself. This is the theme of a contemporary poem by Seifert:

> In stealth, and cautious not to shake
> from eyelashes the trembling dew . . .
> in stealth—no pathos—quietly
> into the night I whisper: You

I

were kinder than those careless nights.
You night of truth, when angels kept
their watch by us, enfolding us;
to your guardian wings of darkness swept.
That cry that rolled through your velvet air!
as between our palms your horror lay;
that dreadful cry, still echoing—
how sweet it sounds to me today!
'PUT OUT THE LIGHTS!' . . . so not to shake
from eyelashes the trembling dew:
in stealth—no pathos—quietly
I whisper: 'Flaming, brilliant through

the blackout, over people shrunk
in terror flared that radiant light. . . .
Far better had the thunder-clap
exploding, split the night!'

The international crisis of 1938 called forth in the Czechs an unusual demonstration of national solidarity. It was, as a young poet wrote, the sight of the great storm raging outside the windows and threatening to destroy the house, which brought home to its inmates, as never before, how precious was the light and warmth within. Suddenly abstract

---

[1] Jen potichu, tak abych nestřás rosu,
jež zachvěla se na konečcích řas,
jen potichu, jen tiše, bez pathosu
té noci říkám: Nebylas

z těch nejstrašnějších. Do perutí strážných
tvé tmy nás prudce zahalil,
ty noci vážná po těch lehkovážných,
anděl, jenž s námi byl.

A pokřik, jenž se válel po tvém plyši,
když hrůzu tvou jsme mnuli ve dlani,
ten strašný křik, jejž podnes kdekdo slyší,
ten zní mi dnes jak sladké volání.

Zhasněte světla! Abych nestřás rosu,
jež zachvěla se na konečcích řas,
jen potichu, jen tiše, bez pathosu
si říkám: Jaký, jaký to byl jas

v té noci, když se všechno zatemnilo
a každý jako stín se schoulil ke kmeni!
Já vím, já vím, že líp by tenkrát bylo
zaslechnout dunění.

ideas like freedom, humanity, and social justice came alive, identified in popular imagination with national interests. Perhaps for the first time in its brief history the Czechoslovak State saw men of all social and political affiliations working together for the common salvation. Among artists, men who had been at odds all their lives joined their voices in a common appeal for support to the international committee of writers. Abandoned by its friends, the State foundered; and Czech literature echoed with defiance and anger for the lost cause. France had been for long the Mecca of Czech artists and the darling of the avantgarde; now at last this one-sided, and rather pathetic love affair ended in disillusion and humiliation. Falling out of love with the West, the Czechs turned back upon themselves. 'What can you do' wrote Karel Čapek, 'it is terribly far from nation to nation: the further we go, the more we are alone. Now better never set foot outside your homeland. Better lock your doors and close your shutters, and let them all do as they like. I no longer care what . . . .'

The political crisis which briefly closed the ranks, brought home to the Czechs the value of all that bound them together—the shared traditions and the common goals which they had inherited from the past. With the enhanced consciousness of cultural continuity, poetry, music, art all acquired a new urgency and a wider appreciation. Like the great bridges of Prague it drew men together, linking past to future, and lending a voice so that the dead could still speak to the living. The dark hour recalled the oldest traditions of the Czech people:

Heard far off are the bells for the peaceful Eve of the Festival.
Through chill evening arises the prayer of the villagers;
And the soul of the Earth is in song; all anguish and faith and sorrow
Are blended in one great hymn, and are soaring
Up to the skies eternal.

Wenceslas, Holy one,
Do not leave it to die into silence
For ourselves, or for men hereafter.[1]

---

[1] Karel Toman, 'Září' ('September'), translated by O. Elton.
Zní zvony z dálky tichým svatvečerem;
modlitba vesnic stoupá chladným šerem.
Duch země zpívá: úzkost, víra, bolest
v jediný chorál slily se a letí
k věčnému nebi.

Svatý Václave,
nedej zahynouti
nám ni budoucím.

So at last like venturers sailing home from distant lands the Czech poets returned to the roots of their national culture. The central theme of poetry was the homeland, and its commonest symbol became that of the prodigal son. The theme was worked out in greatest detail by Hora in a poem '*Jan houslista*' ('Jan the Fiddler'), published in 1939. The book reads like an autobiographical sketch of Hora's own artistic odyssey and it is no coincidence that the initials of the title are the poet's own. A musician Jan, who in his youth had left home to seek better times, returns from abroad after many years of exile. In earlier days he was drawn by the call of distant horizons; now it is home which urgently summons him back. For Jan the road lies backwards not only in space, but also in time: the widower seeks his first sweetheart, the ageing artist his lost childhood. But the hour of return is ill-timed; he comes home to a land filled with uncertainty and tension. And everything is changed from what he remembered: his first love Kate has lost, together with her youth, husband and children. The passage of time, carrying away the familiar landmarks, has divided the former lovers, and they meet as strangers; but as her fingers move over the piano keys, the familiar music awakens forgotten echoes which call them together again:

> A black piano. Katy dressed in black,
> black hair above her forehead braided high.
> So was it that she met her friend come back
> after some twenty years had passed them by.
> His lamp-lit room seemed darkened to her eye.
> 'Autumn? Let us not think of that tonight.'
>
> To play. To take all life between one's hands,
> the rosary of sadness, glistening pearls,
> the flame that changes into tenfold strands
> of sound. To play, and from the mist that swirls
> around one—or from nothing—forge a shield,
> give substance to the dream, lightness to clay,
> voice to the motherland whose lips are sealed
> by hapless fate; when that has passed away,
> to usher in a new Creation Day. . . .
> It was a summer evening. Katy went
> to the open window, from the casement leant
> and gazed into the silence of the night.[1]

---

[1] Translated by E. Osers and J. K. Montgomery.

Je černý klavír. Černé šaty
a černé vlasy nad čelem.

Via memories and dreams, they move back in time from the threatening present to the hopeful past; from winter to spring and the promise of summer. The feeling of home strikes most poignantly at Jan as they walk in the village graveyard. There, surrounded by familiar names, he realizes that now at last he is at home; for what is home but a muster of the familiar dead? From the graves the massed flowers and humming bees are a symbol of life renewed in the eternal cycle of nature—the dead past lives again in present life and future promise. Thus Hora, in the person of Jan, proclaims his faith in time; time no longer the destroyer, but the preserver. As Jan and Kate leave the graveyard, they are besieged by children who beg Jan to play for them. So he takes the fiddle into his hands, and plays. Gravely and attentively the children listen to the music, in a ritual as old and familiar as the movement of trees and the rhythm of the seasons. Art is the medium which links man to man, old life to new, and past to future; crystallizing men's dreams, and giving meaning to all things.

The return of the exile to his home, the poet to his roots, is a poetic allegory which closes a chapter in Czech literary history. To a generation grown old between the wars, the rebellious postures, fanciful styles, and discarded programmes now remained only as symbols of the years in the wilderness: catastrophe had brought them home. In the hard times a small, threatened group must hold fast to that which binds them together—their heritage of history, music, literature—the creations of poets, preserved for a thousand years in the memory of their people.

Tak po dvaceti letech Katy
se setkávala s přítelem
v pokoji jeho setmělém.
'Na podzim myslet? Nechce se mi.'
Hrát . . . Bráti život do svých rukou,
růženec smutku, perlí svit,
plamen, jenž v desaterozvukou
podobu jde se proměnit . . . .
Hrát . . .Z mlhy, z ničeho kout štít,
dát váhu snu, vznos tíze hlíny,
dát hlas rtům němé domoviny,
a třeba po zatracení
jít k novému dni stvoření . . .
Byl jarní večer. Katy vstala
a u okna se zadívala
do plynoucího mlčení.

SELECT BIBLIOGRAPHY

Biebl, K., and Wolker, J., *Listy dvou básníků*, Praha, 1953.
Blahynka, M., and Čutka, J., *Nezval—Wolker*, Ostrava—Brno, 1964.
Čapek, J. B., *Záření ducha a slova*, Praha, 1948.
——, *Profil české poesie a prózy*, Praha, 1947.
Černý, V., *Jaroslav Seifert*, Kladno, 1954.
——, *Zpěv duše*, Praha, 1946.
Chvatík, K., *Bedřich Václavek a vývoj marxistické estetiky*, Praha, 1962.
Deml, J., *Mohyla*, Praha, 1948.
Fischer, O., *Duše, slovo, svět*, Praha, 1965.
Fučík, J., *Stati o literatuře*, Praha, 1951.
Götz, F., *Anarchie v nejmladší české poesii*, Brno, 1922.
——, *Jasníci se horizont*, Praha, 1926.
——, *Básnický dnešek*, Praha, 1931.
Havel, R., and Opelík, J., *Slovník českých spisovatelů*, Praha, 1964.
Honzík, K., *Ze života avantgardy*, Praha, 1963.
Hora, J., *Literatura a politika*, Praha, 1929.
——, *Poesie a život*, Praha, 1959.
Jelínek, A., *Vítězslav Nezval*, Praha, 1961.
Jíša, J., *Česká poezie dvacátých let a básníci sovětského Ruska*, Praha, 1956.
Jíša, J., ed., *Čs.-sovětské literární vztahy v období meziválečném*, Praha, 1965.
Kalista, Z., *Kamarád Wolker*, Praha, 1933.
Konrád, Karel, *O Konstantinu Bieblovi*, Praha, 1952.
Konrad, Kurt, *Ztvárněte skutečnost*, Praha, 1963.
Kratochvíl, L., *Wolker a Nezval*, Praha, 1936.
Kunc, J., *Slovník soudobých českých spisovatelů*, 2 vols., Praha, 1945–6.
Linhart, J., *Jan houslista Josefa Hory*, Praha, 1947.
Marčák, B., *Čas hledání a sporů*, Brno, 1967.
Mukařovský, J., *Kapitoly z české poetiky*, 2 vols., Praha, 1948.
——, *Studie z estetiky*, Praha, 1966.

Nejedlý, Z., ed. Pekárek, V., *O literatuře*, Praha, 1953.

Nezval, V., *Wolker*, Praha, 1925.

Nezval, V., *Moderní básnické směry*, Praha, 1937.

———, ed. Blahynka, M., *Moderní poesie*, Praha, 1958.

———, *Z mého života*, Praha, 1959.

———, *Manifesty, eseje a kritické projevy*, 2 vols., Praha, 1967–8.

Nor, A. C., J. *Wolker, básník a člověk*, Praha, 1947.

Novák, A., *Stručné dějiny literatury české*, Olomouc, 1946.

Opelík, J., ed., *Jak číst poezii*, Praha, 1963.

Pekárek, V., *Wolker—Neumann—Hora*, Praha, 1949.

Píša, A. M., *Směry a cíle*, Praha, 1927.

———, *Proletářská poesie*, Praha, 1936.

———, *Poesie své doby*, Praha, 1940.

———, *Josef Hora*, Praha, 1947.

———, *Soudy, boje a výzvy*, Praha, 1922.

———, *Stopami poezie*, Praha, 1962.

———, Mukařovský, J.; Tomčík, M.; and Závada, V., *Jiří Wolker— příklad naší poesie*, Praha, 1954.

Ripellino, A. M., *Storia della poesia ceca contemporanea*, Rome, 1950.

Šalda, F. X., *O nejmladší poesii české*, Praha, 1928.

———, *Kritické glosy k nové poesii české*, Praha, 1939.

———, *Kritické projevy*, vols. 11–13, Praha, 1959–63.

———, *Studie z české literatury*, Praha, 1961.

Soldan, F., *O Nezvaloři a poválečné generaci*, Praha, 1933.

———, *Tři generace*, Praha, 1940.

———, *J. Wolker*, Praha, 1964.

Sus, O., ed., *Cesty k dnešku*, vol. 2, Brno, 1966.

Svoboda, J., *Přítel V. Nezval*, Praha, 1966.

———, Sixta, J.; and Stýskal, J., *Tři studie o moderní české literatuře*, Praha, 1962.

Štoll, L., *Třicet let*, Praha, 1950.

———, *Z bojů na levé frontě*, Praha, 1964.

Taufer, J., *Vítězslav Nezval*, Praha, 1957.

Teige, K., *Svět, který se směje*, Praha, 1928.

———, *Surrealismus proti proudu*, Praha, 1938.

———, *Svět stavby a básně*, Praha, 1966.

———, *Vývojové proměny v umění*, Praha, 1966.

Urx, E., *V prvních řadách*, Praha, 1962.

Václavek, B., *Od umění k tvorbě*, Praha, 1928.

———, *Poesie v rozpacích*, Praha, 1930.

Václavek, *K problematice současné poesie*, Bratislava, 1934.
———, *Česká literatura XX století*, Praha, 1935.
———, *Tvorbou k realitě*, Praha, 1937.
———, *Literární studie a podobizny*, Praha, 1964.
Wellek, R., *Essays on Czech literature*, The Hague, 1963.
Wolker, J., ed. Píša, A. M., *Listy příteli*, Praha, 1950.
———, *Korespondence s rodiči*, ed. Kuhndel, J., and Wolkrová, Z., Praha, 1952.
Wolkrová, Z., *J. W. ve vzpomínkách své matky*, Praha, 1937.

INDEX

Absurd, cult of the, 39, 44
Acoustics, 47, 101
Acrobats, 39, 60, 79
Alienation, 1, 11, 64, 86, 95–7
Anacoluthon, 85
Anarchy, 2, 14–5, 18, 61, 75, 79, 105, 110, 112
Anglo-American influence, 2, 15, 31, 67, 83
Apocalyptic themes, 17, 55, 111
Apollinaire, G., 9, 16, 30, 66
Architecture, 21, 34, 39, 44, 101
Aragon, L., 107
Arcos, R., 9
Art for Art's sake, 17
Association of ideas, 16, 23, 29–30, 32, 37–8, 45, 47–8, 52, 68–70, 77–9, 96, 101, 103, 105
Audience participation, 37
Austria, 1, 3–4, 8
Automatic texts, 73, 101–2
Avantgarde, 14, 18, 21, 26, 36, 38, 40, 44–9, 53–5, 61, 83–4, 86, 99, 105–6, 108, 114, 117

Bakunin, M., 14
Ballads, 17, 23–6, 46–7, 94
Ballet, 51
Balzac, H. de, 18
Baroque, 1, 65, 81, 96, 99, 113
Baudelaire, C., 2, 15, 65
Bezruč, P., 2
Biblical imagery, see Religious
Biebl, K., 46–8, 77–80, 97, 102, 108, 110
Blok, 107
Bohemia, 51, 53, 76

Bourgeois, 1, 14, 31, 35, 40–1, 108
Brecht, B., 107
Breton, A., 88, 100–1, 107
Březina, O., 2, 6
Brod, M., 9, 107
Brno, 40, 44
Bukharin, N. I., 106–7

Callimachus, 95
Čapek, K., 6, 15–6, 21, 30, 117
Caricature, 9, 34
Carnival, 34, 39, 44, 53, 55, 59
Catholics, 5, 15, 43, 54, 81, 83–4, 87–8, 99, 108, 114
Ceylon, 78
Chaplin, C., 34
Childhood, motifs from, 30–1, 33, 60, 64, 77, 80, 86–7, 96
Childish art, 9, 15–17, 27, 49, 63, 87, 94, 101
Christianity, 18, 20, 87, see also Religion
Cinema, see Films
Circus, 31–2, 35, 60, 67, 85
Clemenceau, G., 4
Clowns, 35, 37, 43
Cocteau, J., 9, 34
Coleridge, S. T., 26
Communal feeling, 6, 11–12, 17, 19, 25–7, 29, 80, 97, 115
Common man, see Popular
Comic strip, 38
Communism, 3, 20–21, 31, 40–1, 84–5
Constructivism, 34, 39, 44, 61, 67, 109
Continuity, cultural, 9, 43, 49, 91, 113–5, 117, 119

Cowboys, 31
Critics and Criticism, 2, 6, 8, 26, 31, 34–5, 37–41, 48–9, 53–4, 58, 61, 64–6, 77, 79, 89–91, 96, 99, 101–2, 105–9, 112–4
Crowd, identification with, see Communal
Cubism, 66

Dada, 6, 36–7, 100, 109
Death, theme of, 12, 30–1, 33, 50–1, 59–60, 63, 66–8, 71–3, 78, 80–3, 85–6, 88–90, 95–9, 111
Decadence, 1–2, 15, 17, 26, 29–30, 83, 88
Deml, J., 54, 87–8
Devětsil, 19, 21–2, 26, 29, 31–4, 40, 65
Dionysus, 61
Discipline in art, 15, 29, 61, 70, 76, 107, 112
Disillusion, 1, 27, 36, 54–5, 80, 84–5
Disk, 26, 37
Dogmatism, 22, 84, 106
Dreams, 2, 15–16, 25, 29–30, 32, 34, 47, 52–3, 57, 62–3, 67, 88, 101–3, 107, 111
Duhamel, G., 9
Durych, J., 43, 54, 83
Dyk, V., 3, 6, 29, 83

Eclecticism, 1
Economic conditions, 1, 4, 15, 21, 49, 82, 84
Edison, 67, 88
Ehrenburg, I., 34, 106–7
Éluard, P., 100
Epic poetry, 66–8, 77, 114
Epicureanism, 39, 46, 67
Escapism, 89–90, 110–111
Expressionism, 9, 15, 17, 27, 54–5, 87, 113

Fairbanks, D., 34
Fairy tales, 15, 27, 30–1, 67, 77, 88
Fantasy, 30, 32, 34, 39, 41, 46, 52, 54, 61, 64–6, 80, 88–9, 93, 96, 100, 105, 107, 110
Fascism, 106–8

Films, 17, 31–2, 34–6, 38–9, 44–5, 66, 101
Forster, E. M., 107
France, 4, 9, 18, 36, 77, 93, 100, 106, 117
Free verse, 30, 87, 102, 112, 114
French influence, 1–2, 8–9, 15, 19, 30, 36, 77, 100–2, 107
Freudism, 33, 61, 85, 96–7, 108
Fronta, 61
Functionalism, 34, 39, 61, 93
Futurism, 6, 15, 109

German influences, 9, 83
Germany, 9, 106, 114
Gide, A., 107, 109
Giotto di Bondone, 66
Goll, I., 34
Götz, F., 21, 26
Graveyard themes, 12, 16, 31, 50–1, 54, 73–4, 81–2, 85–6, 89–91, 98, 119

Halas, F., 61–4, 80–2, 85–8, 90, 94–100, 108–111, 113–4
Hallucinations, 30, 64, 73, 102, 105
Harlequin, 38–9, 47, 53, 55, 85
Heroism, 5, 34, 39, 43, 76
Highbrow art, 31, 36, 66
Hlaváček, K., 2
Hoffmeister, A., 21
Holan, V., 99–100, 110, 114
Hora, J., 9–14, 21, 27, 49–51, 55–8, 70, 79–80, 84, 94–6, 108, 113–5, 118–9
Horace, 95
Hořejší, J., 18–19
Host, 21–2, 26, 38, 40–1
Hrubín, F., 99
Humanism, 3, 5, 18, 21–2, 117
Humour, 35–9, 58–9
Hussites, 4, 18
Huxley, A., 107
Hypnotism, 47, 56, 70, 101

Icarus, 77–8, 97
Iconoclasm, 6, 49, 91
Idealism, 5, 108
Ideology, 4, 27, 31, 39, 46, 49, 54, 64–5, 86, 91, 106, 109

Imagery, *see* Symbolism
Impressionism, 9, 94
Individualism, 5, 27, 29, 43, 61, 100, 108
Irony, 43, 52, 63, 76
Irrational, cult of the, *see* Logic
Italian influence, 6
Italy, 19, 49–51, 93

Jacob, M., 9
Jazz, 17, 45
Journalism, 34, 100, 115
Jugoslavia, 46

Kalista, Dr., Z. 14, 21–2
Karásek, J., 2, 83
Kerensky, 14
Kharkov, 84, 106
Kramař, Dr., K., 5
Kropotkin, Prince P. A., 14

Litoměřice, 114
Lockhart, B., 36
Lenin, 79, 80
Logic, rejection of, 6, 36–7, 39, 61, 70, 90, 100, 103, 108–9
Love poems, 19, 23–5, 33, 35, 45, 47–8, 55, 75, 85–6, 91, 97–8, 110, 118
Lowbrow art, *see* Popular
Lunačarsky, A. V., 65

Mácha, K. H., 113–4
Machar, J. S., 2, 6, 29, 83
Machines, 12, 19, 34, 44
Madonna, 12–13, 16, 50
Magic, 34, 39, 81, 103
Magicians, 32–3, 60, 101
Mallarmé, S., 66, 94
Marienbad, 52
Marseilles, 93
Marxism, 6, 18, 44, 84
Marxists, 8, 84–6, 105, 107, 112
Masaryk, President, T. G., 2–4, 115
Mediterranean, 50, 54, 93
Messiah, 6, 12, 60
Metaphysical themes, 2, 11, 56–7, 94, 100

Metre, 30, 87, 102, 111–2, 114 *see also* Poetics
Modernism, 15, 21, 35, 40, 43, 48, 76, 111–3
Moravia, 2, 21, 87
Moscow, 18, 84, 99, 106–7
Music, 14, 16, 22, 29, 46, 60, 65, 101, 117, 119
Music hall, 31, 37–9
Mysticism, 84, 87–8, 100

Naive art, *see* Childish
Nationalism, 2–3, 5, 14, 41, 112, 113, 115–6
Nativity theme, 12–13, 16
Nature poetry, 2, 8, 51, 55, 87, 114
Nazi Germany, 106
Němcová, B., 113
Neumann, S. K., 2, 6, 8, 41–2, 84, 107, 109
Nezval, V., 26, 29–35, 37–8, 43, 46–8, 51–4, 63–76, 78, 80, 88, 90–1, 93–4, 96, 98–112, 114
Nihilism, 83, 90
Noha, J., 109
Nonsense, cult of, 6, 38 *see also* Logic
Novák, A., 112
Nursery rhymes, 102

Orfeus, 21
Ovid, 95
Owen, W., 19

Pacifism, 3
Painting, 1, 9, 38, 44, 65–6, 95, 98, 101, 104, 108
Paris, 18–19, 33, 44, 54, 70–1, 88, 93, 107
Pásmo, 40, 44
Pasternak, B., 107
Patriotism, 2–3, 15 *see also* Nationalism
Peroutka, F., 5
Personal poetry, 27, 57, 64, 73, 77, 80, 97–8, 110, 112
Philosophy, 12, 17, 36, 39, 56, 65, 73, 83, 95
Phonetics, 101
Photography, 1, 44, 66

Picasso, P., 9, 66
Pictorial composition, 16, 23, 27, 93
Picture poems, 38, 44, 66
Píša, A. M., 37, 43
Poe, E. A., 15, 73
Poetics, 27, 30, 53, 64, 85, 91, 98, 100–102, 110–111
Poetism, 38–9, 41–9, 51, 53–5, 58, 61–7, 73, 76, 79, 85–6, 89, 91, 93–4, 100–2, 113, 115
Politics, 14–15, 17, 21, 54, 84, 90, 109, 112–3, 115–9
Politics and literature, see Socially engaged literature
Polo, E., 17
Popular art, 17, 27, 28, 31, 36, 66
Popular speech, 20, 91, 111
Popular Front, 84, 107
Pragmatism, 6, 83–5
Prague, 14–15, 18–19, 27–8, 30, 36, 67, 73, 84, 93, 103–7, 112, 114–5, 117
Primitivism, 9, 17, 38, 94, 109, 110
Proletarian poetry, 6, 17–31, 34, 36, 39–41, 43, 46–7, 49, 51, 64–5, 80, 84, 99
Proletarian writers, see Rappists
Proletkult, 42
Proletkult movement, 6, 27, 41
Propaganda, 31, 34, 65
Prophet, poet as, 6, 27, 46
Protestantism, 5
Psycho-analysis, 101–2
Publication, conditions of, 1–2, 8, 21, 31, 34, 41–4, 46, 61, 77, 80, 82–3, 115
Prostějov, 14–15
Punctuation, 112 see also Poetics
'Pure' poetry, 39, 47, 65, 70, 94, 100, 110

Radek, K., 107
Rappists, 84, 99, 106
Realism, 5, 17, 27, 38, 43, 62, 80, 89–90, 94, 100, 103, 106–8
Rebels, see Revolution
Reason, rejection of, see Logic
ReD, 65
Religion, 4–6, 54, 64, 84, 87, 114
Religious themes, 12–13, 16–17, 20, 22, 54, 64, 101–2, 117

Religious imagery, 25–6, 32, 62, 68, 75, 86–9, 96, 111
Remarque, E. M., 83
Renaissance, 34
Revolution, 3–4, 14–15, 18–19. 21, 27, 29, 33–4, 36–7, 40, 43, 49, 54, 63, 65, 76, 79, 84–5, 90–1, 95, 97, 105, 108–9, 112
Rhyme, 30, 48, 85, 98, 100, 102, 110
Rilke, R. M., 94
Rimbaud, A., 30
Rococo, 52, 64, 86
Romanticism, 5, 17, 33, 39, 49–50, 52, 65, 77–9, 86–7, 89, 92, 111, 113, 115
Rome, 50, 78, 95 see also Italy
Rondel, 75, 112
Rozhledy, 99
Ruskin, J., 17
Russia, 3–4, 14, 19, 55, 57, 84, 106, see also U.S.S.R.
Rutte, M., 8

Sacco and Vanzetti, 80
Šalda, F. X., 2, 6, 8, 18, 79, 96, 98–9, 114
Scepticism, 36, 43, 98
Sea (as a theme), 26, 45–7, 51, 80
Seifert, J., 19–21, 31–2, 34–6, 38, 40, 44–6, 54–5, 57, 62–3, 80, 84, 91–4, 101, 108, 113–6
Seine, 70
Sentimentality, 17, 44, 47, 99, 115
Serbia, 19
Slovakia, 27
Slovaks, 4
Social themes, 11–13, 16–20, 22–7, 34, 54, 62–3, 80, 83, 94, 97, 105, 109, 112
Socialism, 1, 3–4, 18, 21, 31, 99, 106–7
Socialist realism, 106, 108–9
Socially engaged literature, 17–21, 26–7, 31, 39, 41–3, 54, 62, 83–5, 89–91, 99–100, 106–9, 115, 117
Sokol movement, 15
Sonnet 112, 114
Southern Europe, 11, 50–1, 57
Sova, A., 3
Soviet writers, 106–7; see also U.S.S.R.
Spengler, O., 83

Sport, 39, 44
Šrámek, F., 3, 6, 8
Stream of consciousness, 30, 37, 77
Students, 8, 14, 31
Štyrský, J., 44
Supernatural, 30, 33, 73, 87–8, 96
Surrealism, 6, 30, 44, 61, 77, 79, 88, 100–110
Symbolism, 12, 23–4, 30, 35, 67, 75, 77–9, 85, 87–9, 91, 100, 103–4, 106–7, 109, 116, 119

Taufer, J., 109
Technique, poetic, *see* Poetics
Technology (as a theme), 11, 19, 34–5, 39, 44, 49, 66–7
Teige, K., 19, 21, 26, 31, 34, 38–40, 43, 47, 65–6, 101, 107–8
Time (as a theme), 16, 30–2, 56–7, 95, 113–4, 118–9
Toman, K., 117
Toyen, 98
Translation, 15, 73, 100
Trotsky, L., 3
Typography, 37, 44, 101

Ugliness, cult of, 85, 89, 111
Union café, 14, 15, 19, 21
University of Prague, 14
U.S.S.R., 3–4, 14, 41–3, 54–5, 57, 65, 79, 84, 106–7

Utopianism, 27, 54, 66

Václavek, B., 61
Valéry, P. A., 94
Vančura, V., 21
Var, 26
Vaudeville, *see* Music hall
Venice, 93
Verlaine, P., 2, 15
Vernacular, *see* Popular speech
Verne, J., 31
Vienna, 1, 93
Vildrac, C., 9

War (as a theme), 19, 46, 55, 63, 78, 80–1, 110
War, influence of, 2, 8, 49, 77, 101, 112, 115
Wenceslas, St., 117
Whitman, W., 2
Wilde, O., 15
Wilson, President T. W., 4
Wolker, J., 14–17, 19, 22–9, 31–2, 33–4, 37, 40–1, 43, 46, 62, 80, 94, 99–100

Young Czech Party, 5

Zahradníček, J., 88, 94, 114
Závada, V., 64, 70, 80–1, 86, 88–9, 95, 99, 108, 110, 114
Zhdanov, A. A., 106